Kinderleben oder das Mährchen ohne Ende
The Story Without an End

(on facing page)
Eleanor Vere Boyle: illustration for the Child's Dream. The Story Without an End (London, 1868)

A golden boat on a great, great water.

Friedrich Wilhelm Carové
Kinderleben oder das Mährchen ohne Ende

Sarah Austin
The Story Without an End

Edited and with a Commentary by
Christoph E. Schweitzer

Camden House

Copyright © 1995 by
CAMDEN HOUSE, INC.

Published by Camden House, Inc.
Drawer 2025
Columbia, SC 29202 USA

Printed on acid-free paper.
Binding materials are chosen for strength and
durability.

All Rights Reserved
Printed in the United States of America

ISBN 1-57113-061-6

Library of Congress Cataloging-in-Publication Data

Carove, Friedrich Wilhelm, 1789-1852.
    Kinderleben, oder, Das Märchen ohne Ende - The story without an end / Friedrich Wilhelm Carove; [translated by] Sarah Austin; edited and with a commentary by Christoph E. Schweitzer.
    p. cm. -- (Studies in German literature, linguistics, and culture)
    German and English.
    Includes bibliographical references.
    ISBN 1-57113-061-6
    I. Austin, Sarah, 1793-1867. II. Schweitzer, Christoph E., 1922-. III. Title. IV. Title: Kinderleben. V. Title: Märchen ohne Ende. VI. Title: Story without an end. VII. Series: Studies in German literature, linguistics, and culture
(Unnumbered)
PZ33.C298 1995   94-43844
                                                   CIP

Contents

Preface	vii
Kinderleben oder das Mährchen ohne Ende	1
The Story Without an End	25
Commentary on Carové's Kinderleben oder das Mährchen ohne Ende	49
Commentary on Austin's The Story Without an End	57
The Prefaces	64
The Illustrations	67
Bibliography of the German and English Editions	69

Preface

WHEN I WAS visiting Professor at Yale in the spring of 1980, I tried to establish the identity of the author of a manuscript translation of Goethe's *Hermann und Dorothea*. Jeffrey Sammons suggested Sarah Austin who achieved fame with her translation of Fürst Pückler-Muskau's *Tour in England, Ireland, and France in the Years 1828 and 1829 [...] by a German Prince* (1832). Her three-volume *Characteristics of Goethe* (1833) preceded George Lewes's famous biography of the poet by twenty-two years. While Sarah Austin did not turn out to have been the author of the translation of *Hermann und Dorothea*, her bibliography contained a title that intrigued me: *The Story Without an End* (1834). It was her only translation of a longer literary work, a story by Friedrich Wilhelm Carové entitled *Kinderleben oder das Mährchen ohne Ende* which is contained in his *Moosblüthen* (1830). Carové was a student of Hegel and the author of innumerable philosophic and essayistic treatises. I discovered that there is only one edition of the German original — there are also three editions for the purpose of teaching German — but thirty-one of the English version. Thirteen of them were published in England, the rest in the United States.

Kinderleben oder das Mährchen ohne Ende is a late Romantic *Kunstmärchen* with antecedents in Novalis, Tieck, and E. T. A. Hoffmann. It is unusual in that the only human being, an unnamed child ("das Kind"), lives without any contact with other people; in the course of the story the child learns from various plants and animals. At the end the child decides to stay in nature rather than to go back to the hut where the child had lived.

Carové selected for *Moosblüthen* five vignettes by Philipp Otto Runge who was at the time no longer well known. One of the vignettes immediately precedes *Kinderleben oder das Mährchen ohne Ende* and is with its design directly connected with the story.

Austin first sent the translation to John Murray, the publisher, with a letter that shows her excellent understanding of the uniqueness of the story. The letter is published here for the first time. Ultimately, another publisher took her beautiful English version that captures the spirit of the original and appealed to the anti-materialistic sentiments among the English-reading public. Among the editors of the English version, A. Bronson Alcott is the most interesting one. He sees in the child's experiences an "Emblem Of The Spiritual Life." Carové's ideas are close to those of transcendentalism, a movement of which Alcott was a prominent member. The reader will find Alcott's preface in this volume.

Eight artists tried their hand at illustrating the story: among them Eleanor Vere Boyle and Frank C. Papé were clearly the best. I discuss briefly the work of each illustrator and then conclude the volume with a list of the thirty-one editions that I have been able to ascertain.

I want to thank the National Endowment for the Humanities for a grant that enabled me to look at letters by Sarah Austin in London and Weimar, the many libraries in this country, and the British Library for giving me valuable information about the editions. Specifically, I want to thank the Staatsbibliothek zu Berlin Preussischer Kulturbesitz for authorizing me to publish *Kinderleben oder das Märchen ohne Ende* and John Murray, for authorizing me to publish Sarah Austin's letter, mentioned above. Last but not least, I want to thank James Hardin who again took on a challenging task when accepting this manuscript.

*Vignette by Philipp Otto Runge.
Originally published in Ludwig* Tieck's Minnelieder aus dem schwäbischen Zeitalter

Friedrich Wilhelm Carové

Kinderleben oder das Mährchen ohne Ende

I.

Es war einmal ein Kind, das wohnte in einer engen Hütte, aber in der Hütte war nichts als ein kleines Bettchen, und in einer dunkeln Ecke hing ein Spiegel. Das Kind kümmerte sich aber nicht um den Spiegel, sondern sobald der erste Sonnenstrahl leise durch die runden Scheiben schlüpfte, und des Kindes Augenlieder küßte, und draußen das Finklein und Zeiserlein ihr Morgenlied anstimmten, und das Kind freundlich aufweckten, ging es hinaus auf die Wiese, und forderte von der Schlüsselblume Mehl, und Zucker von dem Veilchen, und von der Butterblume Butter, schöpfte in einem blauem Blumenkelche Thautropfen von den Maßlieben, breitete ein großes Lindenblatt aus, setzte seine kleinen Näschereien darauf und labte sich daran. Zuweilen lud es eine summende Biene, öfter doch die bunten Schmetterlinge, am liebsten die blauen Libellen zu Gast. Die Biene murmelte vieles von ihren Reichthümern durch den Bart; das Kind aber meinte, der aufgespeicherten Schätze werde sie doch nicht recht froh, und es müsse ihr doch viel herrlicher zu Muthe seyn, wenn sie in der freien Frühlingsluft herumschwebe, und zum Gewebe der Sonnenstrahlen fröhlich summen könne, als wenn sie mit schweren Füßen und schwerem Herzen ihr Wachssilber und ihr Honiggold in die enge dunkle Zelle einschleppe. Darin gab ihm der Schmetterling Beifall und erzählte, wie er sonst so begierlich gewesen sey; wie er nur an das Essen gedacht und nicht ein einzigmal nach dem blauen Himmel aufgeschaut habe. Endlich sey er aber in *sich* gegangen, und — wie er sonst halb träumend auf der schmutzigen Erde schwerfällig herumgekrochen, so sey er nach kurzer Zeit auf einmal wie aus einem schweren Schlafe erwacht, und ganz verändert gewesen. Nun könne er in der Luft gehen, und habe jetzt seine einzige Freude daran, bald mit dem Lichte zu spielen und den Himmel in seinen Flügelaugen zu spiegeln, bald dem stillen Gespräche der Blumen zuzuhören und ihre Geheimnisse zu belauschen. Das gefiel dem Kinde wohl, und sein Mahl mundete ihm noch so gut, und der Sonnenglanz auf Blättern und Blumen schien ihm noch so heiter und erquicklich. Wenn aber die Biene wieder auf die Bettelei, und der Schmetterling auch bald wieder fort zu seinen Spielgesellen geflattert war, dann saß noch die Libelle auf einem Grashalm, und ihr schlankes, blankes Leibchen liebäugelte mit der Sonne, und war selbst glänzender blau als der Himmel, und die zwei Flügelpaare neckten die Blumen, weil sie nicht auch davon fliegen könnten, sondern dem Sturm und dem Regen still halten müßten. Die Libelle aber nippte nur ein wenig an einem hellen Thautropfen und an dem blauen Veilchenhonig, und lispelte dann geflügelte Worte. Da hörte das Kind auf, sich an den Näschereien zu belustigen, schloß die dunkelblauen Augen und horchte mit geneigtem Köpflein dem süßen Gekose. Denn die Libelle erzählte Vieles vom frohen Leben im grünen Walde; wie sie bald mit ihren Gespielen Versteckens spiele hinter den Blättern der Buche und Eiche, und Nachläufchens über den stillen Wässern, bald ruhig den Sonnenstrahlen zusehe, die von Moos zu Kräutern, von Kräutern zu Gesträuchen emsig eilten und überall Licht und Wärme austheilten. Nachts aber schleiche der Mondschein herum und tröpfle den dürstenden Blumen Thau in den Mund, und wenn frühe das Morgenroth zarte Himmelsrosen auf die Schlummernden herabwerfe, um sie damit zu wecken und zu necken, dann lachten, halb trunken, die Blumen sich an, die meisten aber könnten das schwere Köpfchen noch lange nicht ganz aufheben. So erzählte die Libelle, und weil das Kind noch unbeweglich auf sein Händchen gestützt da saß mit geschlossenen Augen, vermeinte sie, es wäre eingeschlummert; schwang also ihr doppelt Flügelpaar und flog gesättigt dem rauschenden Walde zu.

II.

DAS KIND WAR aber nur in ein wonniges Träumen versunken und wäre gar zu gerne Sonnenstrahl und Mondschein gewesen, — und hätte noch immer mehr und mehr zuhorchen mögen. Als nun Alles still war und still blieb, schlug es die Augen auf und sah sich um nach seinem lieben Gaste. Der aber war wieder in die weite Welt geflogen. Da mochte es auch nicht länger allein da sitzen, stand auf und ging hinunter an den rieselnden Bach. Der wellte und quellte so recht lustig dahin, und tummelte sich gar possierlich, um über Hals und Kopf sich in den Strom zu stürzen, gerade als folge der schwere Berg ihm auf der Ferse nach, dem er vor kurzem erst entronnen und nur mit einem lebensgefährlichen Sprunge entwischt war. Da ließ sich das Kind mit den Wellen in ein Gespräch ein und fragte sie, wo sie her kämen? Sie wollten ihm aber lange nicht Antwort stehen, sondern purzelten übereinander weg, bis endlich ein crystallhelles Wellchen hinter einem Steine sich niederließ, um das freundliche Kind nicht zu betrüben. Von ihm hörte das Kind sehr seltsame Geschichten, die es aber nicht alle verstand; denn es gab ihm Kunde von seinen früheren Schicksalen und vom Innern des Berges. Vor langen Zeiten, sagte es, wohnte ich mit unzähligen Geschwistern im großen Weltmeer zusammen in Frieden und Einigkeit. Wir trieben mancherlei Kurzweil, stiegen bald häuserhoch in die Höhe, und guckten nach den Sternen, bald ließen wir uns hinunterplumpsen tief — tief hinab, und schauten zu, wie die Korallen sich müd arbeiteten, um endlich einmal an das liebe Tageslicht zu kommen. Ich aber war hoffärtig und dünkte mich viel besser als meine Geschwister. Als daher die Sonne einmal wieder in's Meer hineinstach, hing ich mich fest an einen heißen Strahl, und dachte nun auch zu den Sternen zu kommen und einer ihres Gleichen zu werden. War aber noch gar nicht weit hinaufgestiegen, als der Strahl mich abschüttelte, und mich, mir nichts, dir nichts, auf eine finstere Wolke niederfallen ließ. Bald zuckte Feuer durch die Wolke, und ich schwebte in großer Lebensgefahr; doch die ganze Wolke ließ sich auf einen Berg nieder, und so kam ich mit der Angst und einem blauen Auge davon. Nun hoffte ich geborgen zu seyn, als ich auf einmal auf einem Kiesel ausglitt, von einem Steine aus den andern fiel, immer tiefer in den Berg hinein, bis es endlich stockfinster wurde, und ich nichts mehr hörte, noch sah. Da fühlte ich wohl, der Hochmuth komme vor dem Fall, ergab mich gelassen meinem Schicksal, und wie ich schon auf der Wolke allen herben Stolz abgelegt hatte, so ward mir hier nun auch das Salz der Demuth zu Theil, und — nach vielen Läuterungen durch die geheimnißvollen Kräfte der Metalle und Steine, durfte ich endlich wieder in die freie heitere Luft hinaus. Nun will ich zu meinen Geschwistern in das Weltmeer zurück, und dann geduldig warten, bis ich zu etwas Besserem berufen werde. — Es hatte aber kaum ausgeredet, als die Wurzel eines Vergißmeinnichtchens das Wellchen beim Schopf faßte und es einsog, auf daß es zum Blümlein werde und als blaues Sternlein freundlich glänze an dem grünen Firmament der Erde.

III.

Das Kind wußte nicht recht, was es zu allem dem sagen sollte; sinnend ging es zurück, legte sich in sein Bettchen und träumte die ganze Nacht von dem Meer und den Sternen und dem dunkelen Berge. Der Mond aber betrachtete gar zu gerne das schlummernde Kind, wie es mit dem Köpflein auf das rechte Aermchen sanft hingelehnt dalag. Er blieb lange vor dem kleinen Fenster stehen und ging nur zögernd weiter, um auch einigen Kranken das dunkle Kämmerlein zu erhellen. Wie nun des Mondes sanftes Licht auf des Kindes Augen ruhte, kam es ihm vor, als sitze es in einem goldenen Kahne auf einem großen, großen Wasser; unzählige Sterne schwammen schimmernd auf dem tief dunkeln Spiegel. Es streckte sein Händchen nach dem nächsten Sternlein aus; aber wie es dasselbe berührte, war es verschwunden, und das Wasser spritzte ihm entgegen. Da merkte es wohl, daß das nicht die rechten Sterne wären, sah hinauf zum Himmel, und wäre gern hinaufgeflogen. Während dem aber war der Mond seines Weges gewandert, und da wurde das Kind von dem Traume hinauf in die Wolken getragen, und es vermeinte, auf einem weißen Schäflein zu sitzen und viele, viele Lämmlein ringsum weiden zu sehen. Es griff nach einem Lämmlein, um mit ihm zu spielen, da war es nur Dunst und Nebel, und das Kind ward betrübt und wünschte sich wieder hinunter auf seine Wiese, wo sein Schäfchen lustig herumsprang. Unterdessen war der Mond hinter den Berg schlafen gegangen und ringsum Alles dunkel geworden. Da fiel das Kind in den finstern Berg hinab und erschrak so darüber, daß es plötzlich erwachte, als eben auch auf dem nächsten Hügel der Morgen seine himmelhellen Augen aufschlug.

IV.

Das Kind raffte sich auf und ging, um sich von seinem Schrecken zu erholen, in das Blumengärtlein hinter dem Hüttchen, wo die Beete noch von vielen Jahren her mit Palm eingefaßt standen, und wo es wußte, daß ihm alle Blumen freundlich entgegen nicken würden, wenn gleich die *Tulipane* die Nase gar zu hoch trug, und die *Ranunkel* einen steifen Hals zur Ausrede nahm, um ihm den Morgengruß nicht zunicken zu müssen. Die *Rose* mit ihren vollen Wangen lächelte und grüßte das Kind am heitersten; darum ging es zu ihr hin und küßte sie auf den duftenden Mund. Da klagte die Rose zärtlich, daß das Kind so selten in den Garten komme. So dufte und glühe sie vergebens den lieben langen Tag; denn die andern Blumen sähen sie entweder nicht, weil sie zu niedrig ständen, oder wären selbst des Duftes und der Glut zu reich. Sie aber freue sich am mehrsten, wenn sie sich in einem blühenden Kindesköpfchen spiegeln und ihm in den süßen Düften ihre Herzensgeheimnisse anvertrauen könne. Unter andern sagte die Rose dem Kinde in's Ohr: "sie sey die Fülle der Gegenwart." Und wirklich schien das Kind ganz das Weitergehen vergessen zu haben, als der blaue *Rittersporn* ihm zurief, ob es denn gar nichts mehr auf seinen alten treuen Freund halte; der bleibe blau einmal wie das andremal, und wenn er einmal todt wäre, werde er es doch noch immer mit blauen Augen ansehen. Das Kind dankte für seine Treuherzigkeit und ging dann weiter zur Hyacinthe, neben der viele pausbäckige, buntschillernde Tulpen standen. Schon von weitem schickte die *Hyacinthe* dem Kinde Kußhändchen entgegen, denn sie wußte sich nicht zu lassen vor Liebe. War sie nun gleich nicht besonders schön, so fühlte das Kind sich doch wundersam zu ihr hingezogen, denn es meinte, so heiß und inbrünstig werde es von keiner Blume geliebt. Die Hyacinthe aber ergoß ihr volles Herz und weinte auch sehr, weil sie so einsam dastehe; die *Tulpen* seyen zwar ihre Landsleute, aber so kalt und unempfindlich, daß sie sich ihrer fast schämen müsse. Das Kind sprach ihr zu, und meinte, so arg sey es doch wohl nicht; die Tulpen sprächen ihre Liebe aus in farbigen Blikken, wenn sie, die Hyacinthe, in duftigen Worten rede; diese seyen zwar schöner und verständlicher, aber jene müsse man darum doch nicht gering achten. Da gab sich die Hyacinthe zufrieden und das Kind ging hin zu den bestäubten *Aurikeln*, die gar gutmüthig aus ihrer Demuth zu ihm hinaufsahen und so gern ihm noch mehr gegeben hätten, wenn sie selbst nicht so arm gewesen wären. Aber dem Kinde genügte ihr züchtiger Gruß; es fühlte sich ja selbst noch so arm und erkannte auch hinter dem gelblichten Staub die dunkeln sinnigen Farben. Doch die bescheidnen Aurikeln schickten selbst das Kind zu der nahen *Lilie*, die sie gern als ihre Königin verehrten. Und als das Kind zur Lilie kam, da schwankte die schlanke Blume, und neigte in gesänftigtem Stolz und in erhobener Demuth das blasse, länglichte Antlitz, und duftete dem Kind einen sehnsuchtsvollen Gruß entgegen. Das Kind wußte nicht, wie ihm geschah. Es durchströmte sein Inneres, daß seine Aeuglein feucht wurden; denn es sah, wie die Lilie mit klarem Auge auf zur Sonne, und die Sonne wieder herab in die Tiefe des reinen Kelches schaute, und in diesem Wechselschauen alle die goldenen Staubfäden sich in einer Mitte vereinigten, und es hörte, wie ein rothes Herrgottsthierchen auf dem Boden des Kelches zum andern sprach: "weißt du auch, daß wir in der Blume des Himmels wohnen?" und das andre erwiederte: "Ja, und jetzt wird das Geheimniß vollbracht!" Und wie das Kind dies alles sah und hörte, flog eine Ahndung von seinen unbekannten Eltern, wie in einen Heiligenschimmer gehüllt, an seinen Augen vorüber. Es wollte darnach haschen, aber fort war der Schimmer und das Kind glitt aus, und wäre beinahe gefallen, wenn ein Johannesbeerstrauch es nicht aufgefangen hätte. Da erhoben die rothen Beeren ein lautes Geschrei; denn sie meinten, das Kind sey der kleine Johannes und jede wollte zuerst von ihrem Herrn genossen seyn, vielleicht in der Hoffnung, zum Rubine im Himmelsgarten zu werden. Das Kind brach sich einige der kleinen Marktschreier zum Morgenbrod und als die übrigen sich nicht zufrieden geben wollten, eilte es zurück in sein Hüttchen um den übrigen keine abschlägige Antwort geben zu müssen.

V.

Aber in dem Hüttchen war nicht lange seines Bleibens; es war so trüb und enge und still darin, und draußen schien alles zu lachen und zu jubeln in der Klarheit und unbeschränkten Weite. Darum ging das Kind hinaus in den grünen Wald, von dem schon die Libelle ihm soviel Anmuthiges gesagt hatte. Es fand aber alles noch weit schöner und lieblicher. Denn überall, wo es hinging, küßten die zarten Moose ihm die Füßlein, und die Gräser umfaßten seine Kniee, und die Blumen küßten das Händchen, ja selbst die Sträucher strichen ihm freundlich und kühlend über die Wangen und die hohen Bäume nahmen es auf in ihren duftigen Schatten. Da war der Lust kein Ende. Die kleinen Waldvögelein pfiffen und sangen, so gut sie konnten, und hüpften und flatterten gar fröhlich durcheinander, und die kleinen Waldblümelein blühten und dufteten um die Wette, und jeder Wohlklang nahm einen Wohlgeruch bei der Hand, und so spatzierten sie herein in des Kindleins Herz und hielten dort einen lieblustigen Hochzeitstanz. Aber die Nachtigall und die Maiblume tanzten vor; denn die Nachtigall "sang nichts als Liebe," und die Maiblume athmete nichts als Unschuld, und jene war Bräutigam und diese war Braut. Und die Nachtigall konnte nicht satt werden, das Nämliche hundertmal zu sagen, weil die Liebe immer neu aus dem Herzen herausquoll; und die Maiblume neigte sich verschämt, damit man ihr glühendes Herzlein nicht sehe. Doch lebte jedes so sehr nur einzig und allein in dem andern, daß man nicht wußte, waren die Töne der Nachtigall fliegende Maiblumen, oder die Maiblumen sichtbare, als Tropfen herabgethaute, Nachtigalltöne. Das Kind war freudenvoll. Es setzte sich nieder, und meinte schier, es müsse auch Wurzeln schlagen und wohnen bleiben unter dem kleinen Pflanzenvolke, um dann an allen ihren zarten Freuden noch weit inniger Theil nehmen zu können. Denn es hatte sein inniges Wohlgefallen an dem heimlichen, still dämmernden Leben der Moose und Heidekräuter, die nichts vom Sturm und nichts vom Frost, noch vom Sonnenbrand erfuhren, sondern sich mit ihren vielen Nachbarn und Freunden wohl seyn ließen, und sich friedlich und gesellig labten an dem Thau und dem Schatten, die ihnen von höheren Gewächsen gespendet wurden. Für sie auch war es jedesmal ein großes Fest, wenn ein Sonnenstrahl sie heimsuchte, während die Wipfel der großen Bäume sich nur am purpurnen Morgen- und Abendstrahl besonders freuten und ergötzten.

VI.

UND WIE DAS Kind da saß, da raschelte aus den dürren Blättern vom vorigen Jahre ein Mäuslein hervor, und aus der Ritze eines Felsens schlüpfte ein Eidechslein halb heraus, und beide schauten vorwitzig mit den glashellen Aeuglein nach dem kleinen Fremdling, und als sie sahen, daß er keine Schelmerei im Schilde führe, faßten sie Muth und kamen näher herbei. "Möchte wohl bei euch wohnen!" sprach, um sie nicht zu erschrecken, mit sanfter, zurückgehaltener Stimme das Kind zu den zwei Thierchen. "Eure Kämmerlein sind so heimlich, so warm und auch so kühlig, und die Blumen wachsen euch zu den Fenstern herein, und die Vögel singen euch das Morgenlied, und pfeifen euch zu Tisch und Bett." — "Ja," entgegnete das Mäuslein, "es wäre schon alles gut, wenn nur die Kräuter — statt der dummen Blumen — lauter Haselnüsse und Buchecker trügen und ich nicht im Frühling unten an ihren bittern Wurzeln nagen müßte, während sie vor der Welt mit ihren Blumen süß thun und sich breiten und brüsten, als wenn sie des Honigs die Hülle und Fülle im Keller hätten." — "Schweige doch," fiel das Eidechslein dem Mäuslein schnippisch in die Rede; "weil du grau bist, so meinst du, es sollten auch andere ehrliche Leute ihre schönen Kleider wegwerfen, oder etwa in der finstern Erdkiste liegen lassen, und immer nur grau tragen. Ich bin nicht so neidisch. Meinethalben können die Blumen sich putzen, wie sie wollen, es kostet sie ihr Geld, und es nähren sich doch Bienen und Käfer von den Blumen. Aber was die Vögel in der Welt thun, das weiß ich nicht. Das ist ein Geplauder und Geplapper von Morgens früh bis Abends spät, daß einem Hören und Sehen vergeht, und das einen Tag wie den andern. Und sie thun und arbeiten nichts, und schnappen nur Unsereinem die Fliegen und Spinnchen vor dem Munde weg. Ich für meinen Theil könnte leiden, daß alle Vögel mit einemmal Käfer und Fliegen würden!" — Dem Kind wurde kalt und wieder warm, wie es die bösen Zungen so dreschen hörte. Es konnte nicht begreifen, wie man die sinnigen Blumen dumm schelten und den unschuldigen, lieblichen Vöglein so Böses nachreden könne. Es war wie aus einem schönen Traume aufgeschreckt, und der Wald bedünkte ihm einsam und öde, und es wurde ihm ganz unheimlich zu Muth. Rasch stand es auf, daß die Eidechse und das Mäuslein erschrocken zurückfuhren, und sich nicht umsahen, bis sie sich vor dem großen Fremdling mit den großen unwilligen Augen gesichert hielten.

VII.

Das Kind aber ging von dannen, und, weil es nachdenklich das Köpfchen senkte, merkte es nicht, daß es den unrechten Fußpfad einschlug, und sah nicht, wie die Blumen es auf beiden Seiten nikkend bewillkommten, und hörte nicht, wie die alten Vöglein von den Zweigen und die jungen aus den Nestern ihm zuriefen: "Gott grüß dich, du unser lieber kleiner Königssohn." Es ging und ging immer weiter in den Wald hinein, und konnte noch immer nicht klug werden aus dem wirren und wüsten Gerede der zwei aberwitzigen Plaudertaschen. Es hätte alles vergessen mögen, und konnte doch nicht. Vielmehr verwickelte es sich immer mehr in das tückische Spinnengewebe, und fast wären die Augen ihm übergegangen. Da kam es plötzlich an ein stilles Wasser, über dem sich junge Buchen freundlich mit Armen umfingen. Es sah hinein und sein Blick war wie von einem Zauber festgebunden. Es mußte stehen bleiben und schauen in den mild erhellten Spiegel, aus dessen Tiefe das zartgrünende Laub der jungen Buchen und dazwischen hindurch des Himmels freundliches Blau so wundersam heraufglänzten. Vergessen war die Betrübniß, und verhallt war das Echo des Mißklanges in seinem Innern. Das Herzlein war hinauf in die Augen gestiegen und gern hätte es das sanfte Farbenbild eingesogen, oder wäre aus sich selbst in die liebliche Tiefe hinabgesunken. Da fing die Luft in den Wipfeln zu säuseln an. Das Kind schlug die Augen auf und sah oben das schimmernde Grün und das Blaue, und wußte nicht, ob es wachte oder träumte. War *oben*, oder war *unten* in der Tiefe das wahre Laub und der wahre Himmel? War das Untere für das Obere, oder war die Höhe der Tiefe zu lieb da? — Lange schwankte das Kind, und wonnig träumend wogten zwischen Beiden seine Gedanken, als in liebender Hast die Libelle herbeiflog, und schwirrend ihren freundlichen Wirth begrüßte. Das Kind dankte lächelnd, und war ordentlich froh, einen Bekannten zu treffen, mit dem es das volle Mahl seiner Freude theilen konnte. Aber vor allen Dingen fragte es die Libelle, ob es ihm wohl über das Oben und Unten, über Höhe und Tiefe Bescheid geben könne? — Die Libelle flog hinauf und flog hinunter; doch das Wasser sprach: "Das Laub und der Himmel da droben sind nicht die wahren; das Laub welkt und fällt ab, und der Himmel umwölkt sich oft und wird zuweilen sogar ganz finster." Das Laub und der Himmel aber sprachen: "Das Wasser äfft uns nur nach und muß die Bilder verändern nach unserm Belieben und kann keines festhalten." — Da merkte die Libelle, daß das Oben und das Unten nur in den Augen des Kindes *für einander* daseyen, und daß das Laub und die Bilder und der Himmel nur in den Gedanken des Kindes wahr und wirklich seyen, weil das Kind sie festhalten und mit sich forttragen könne. Das sagte sie dem Kindlein, aber mahnte es zugleich zur Rückkehr an, da die Blätter in der Abendluft schon den Zapfenstreich trommelten, und in allen Ecken nacheinander die Lichter ausgelöscht würden. Als nun das Kind ihm bestürzt gestand, daß es den Rückweg schwerlich finden werde, und auch fürchte, die dunkle Nacht möchte über es herfallen, wenn es allein heimgehe, da flog die Libelle vor ihm her und zeigte ihm eine Felsenhöhle, worin es übernachten könne, und das Kind war dessen wohl zufrieden, weil es auch gerne gewußt hätte, wie es sich außer seinem gewohnten Bettchen schlafen lasse.

VIII.

DIE LIBELLE ABER war wegsam und regsam, und die Dankbarkeit stärkte ihre Flügel, damit sie ihrem Gaste auch die gebührende Ehre beweise. Doch in der Dämmerung war guter Rath theuer. Sie schwirrte hin und her, ohne recht zu wissen, was zu thun sey, als sie bei dem letzten fortfliegenden Sonnenstrahl am Abhang der Höhle einige Erdbeeren glänzen sah, die so viel Abendroth getrunken hatten, daß der Kopf ihnen ganz schwer war. Da flog sie zu einer Glockenblume, die nahe dabei stand, und raunte ihr in's Ohr, der Herr und König aller Blumen sey im Walde, und der müsse nach Würden geehrt werden. Die Aglaye ließ sich das nicht zweimal sagen, sondern fing mit Macht an zu läuten, und als ihre Nachbarin das hörte, läutete sie auch, und bald waren alle Blumenglocken groß und klein in Bewegung und läuteten, als sollte die königliche Erde selbst mit einem kaiserlichen Kometen=Prinzen Hochzeit halten. Die blauen Glocken tönten tief, und die weißen hoch und hell, und alle klungen lieblich in einander. Aber die Vögel wurden nicht wach in ihren hohen Nestern, und den andern Thieren waren die Ohren nicht fein genug, oder zu sehr mit Haaren verwachsen. Nur die Johannisfünklein vernahmen das Festgeläute, weil sie mit den Blumen durch das Licht Geschwisterkinder waren. Sie fragten bei ihren nächsten Verwandten, den Maiblumen, und erfuhren von ihnen, daß eine große Blume den Fußsteig hinaufgegangen sey, welche noch weit schöner blühe, als die Rose, und zwei Sterne trüge, die noch weit lieblicher glühten, als die Johannisfunken; und das müsse wohl ihr aller König seyn. Da flogen alle Fünklein den Fußpfad entlang, und suchten und suchten, und kamen endlich, wie die Libelle es gehofft hatte, an die Höhle. Als sie nun das Kind gewahrten, und jedes sich in seinen Augen gedoppelt wiedersah, da frohlockten sie, riefen alle Uebrigen herbei, setzten sich ringsumher auf das Gesträuche, und bald war es so hell an der Höhle, daß Gras und Kräuter zu wachsen anfingen, als wäre es voller Tag. Nun hatte die Libelle gewonnen Spiel. Das Kind war hocherfreut über das schöne Blumengeläute und die vielen kleinen hellaugigen Gesellen, und konnte obendrein sich Erdbeeren zum Abendbrod pflücken.

IX.

Als es sich zur Genüge gelabt hatte, setzte es sich hin auf das weiche Moos, schlug die Beinchen übereinander, und fing an mit den Johannisfünklein zu plaudern, und weil es selbst so oft an seine unbekannten Eltern dachte, fragte es auch sie, wer denn wohl ihre Eltern seyen? — Das zunächstsitzende gab ihm Bescheid und erzählte: Sie seyen früher Pflanzen gewesen; aber keine von denen, die nur ihre Wurzelhände gierig in den Boden senkten und nur aus der dunkeln Erde ihre Nahrung an sich zögen, um nur recht dick und fett zu werden, sondern das Licht sey ihnen lieber gewesen, als alles, und während die andern Blumen Nachts geschlafen, hätten sie unermüdet nach dem Lichte geschaut, und es eingesogen mit frommer Sehnsucht — Sonnen= und Mond= und Sternenlicht. Und das Licht habe sie innerlich geläutert, daß sie nicht wie die gelben Erdblumen giftige Milch erzeugt hätten, sondern süße Düfte für kranke, sehnsuchtsvolle Herzen, und kraftreiches ätherisches Oel zum Balsam für arme Kranke und Verwundete. Als daher ihr Herbst gekommen, seyen sie nicht mit Haut und Haar, wie die anderen, erdetrunken, auch hinabgesunken in den finstern Erdengrund, sondern hätten vollends ihr erdiges Kleid abgeschüttelt, und wären frank und frei in die Höhe gestiegen. Da sey es aber so außerordentlich hell gewesen, daß ihnen das Gesicht vergangen, und als sie wieder zu sich gekommen, hätten sie als Johannisfünklein auf einem dürren Blumenstiel gesessen. — Nun gefielen die Fünklein dem Kindlein noch einmal so wohl, und es plauderte noch eine Weile mit ihnen, und erfuhr auch, warum ihrer im Frühlinge so viele zum Vorschein kämen; das geschehe, um durch den grüngoldigen Glanz auch die zurückgebliebenen Blumengeschwister zur Lichtliebe zu locken.

X.

Während dieser Zwiegespräche hatte die Libelle auch für das Schlafgemach ihres Gastes gesorgt. Das Moos, auf dem das Kind saß, war hinter seinem Rücken vor Freude ellenhoch gewachsen, die Libelle aber war mit ihren Schwestern so darauf herumgedämmert, daß es sich langes Weges in die Höhle niedergestreckt hatte. Alle Spinnen aber aus der ganzen Nachbarschaft hatte die Libelle aus dem Schlafe aufgestört, und als diese die Helle gesehen, hatten sie so fleißig gewoben, daß ihr Gewebe wie ein Vorhang vor der Höhle herabhing. Wie nun das Sandmännchen dem Kinde kleine Aeuglein machte, und es die Fünklein bat, sich nun nicht weiter in ihren Spielen um seinetwillen aufhalten zu lassen, hob die Libelle mit ihren Schwestern den Vorhang in die Höhe, bis das Kind zur Ruhe gegangen war, und ließen ihn dann wieder fallen, damit die heimtückischen Mücken nicht ungezupft und ungerupft in die Höhle hineinkommen und den kleinen Schläfling nicht beunruhigen könnten. Das Kind legte sich nun zwar auf sein rechtes Oehrchen, um zu schlafen, denn es war recht müde geworden; allein schlafen konnte es doch nicht, denn das Mooslager war doch etwas anders, als sein Bettchen, und die Höhle war ihm auch noch gar so fremd. Es legte sich links und wieder rechts, und als es mit dem Schlafen gar nicht gehen wollte, richtete es sich auf, um zu warten, bis es dem Herrn Schlaf gefällig wäre zu kommen. Aber wer nicht kam, das war der Schlaf, und wer im ganzen Walde bald allein noch wachte, das war das Kind. Denn die Blumen hatten sich müde geläutet, und die Fünklein müde geflogen, und selbst die Libelle, die vor der Höhle wachen wollte, fiel bald aus dem Nicken in's Schlafen. Immer stiller wurde es im Walde; hier und dort fiel noch ein dürres Blatt, das von einem frischen aus seiner alten Wohnung vertrieben wurde; dort und hier hörte man ein junges Vöglein pipen, wenn seine Alten es im Schlaf etwas drückten; und nur zuweilen summste eine Mücke einige Augenblicke in dem Vorhang, bis eine Spinne auf den Zehen herbeischlich, und ihr die Kehle so zuschnürte, daß ihr nicht bloß das Summen und Brummen, sondern auch Sehen und Hören für immer verging. Und je stiller es wurde, desto mehr horchte das Kind, und ihm schauerte, wenn es wieder etwas hörte. Endlich war alles mäuschenstill im Walde, als sollte nie mehr etwas erwachen. Das Kind bog sich weiter hervor, um zu sehen, ob es denn auch draußen ganz so dunkel sey, wie in der Höhle, und es sah nichts, als die stockfinstre Nacht, die Alles in ihren dichten Schleier eingehüllt hatte. Doch, — als es auch nach Oben hinschaute, begegneten ihm die freundlichen Blicke einiger Sterne, und überraschten es auf das Freudigste. Denn es fühlte sich jetzt doch nicht mehr so ganz allein. Waren gleich die Sterne so weit, weit weg, so wußte es doch von ihnen, und sie wußten von ihm, denn sie schauten ihm ja Auge in Auge. Das Kind vertiefte sich in den Anblick, und es war ihm, als müsse es hinauffliegen aus der dunkelen Höhle — dahin, wo die Sterne so rein und heiter strahlten, und es fühlte sich recht arm gegen ihren Glanz, und wie gebunden und gefangen gegen ihr freies Schweben und Schweifen.

XI.

ABER DIE STERNE zogen vorüber und ließen dem Kinde nur noch eine kleine Weile ihr schimmerndes Bild in den Augen. Auch dieses zerrann, und das Kind wollte sich eben ermüdet niederlegen, als hinter einem Busche hervor vom stillen Wasser her ein zitternd *Irrlicht* zum Vorschein kam, daß das Kind zuerst meinte, einer der Sterne hätte einen Umweg genommen, es zu besuchen und mit sich hinaufzunehmen. Und vor Freude und Erstaunen athmete das Kind tief auf, und da kam auch das Irrlicht ganz nahe heran und ließ sich nieder auf einen feuchten bemoosten Stein vor der Höhle, und ein anderes flakkerte rasch hinter ihm drein und setzte sich diesem gegenüber und seufzte, wie aus hohler Brust: "Nun Gott sey Dank, daß ich endlich einmal ausruhen darf!" "Ja," sprach das andere, "dank' es dem unschuldigen Kinde da drinnen, das uns mit seinem reinen Othem angezogen hat." — "Seyd ihr denn," fragte zögernd das Kind, "nicht von jenen Sternen, die da oben so freudig leuchten und wandeln?" — "Ja, wären wir Sterne," erwiederte das erste, "wir zögen ruhig unsre Bahn in dem heitern Elemente, und ließen unbekümmert diesen Wald und die ganze Erde links liegen;" — "und bräuchten nicht," fiel das zweite ihm in's Wort, "an den schalen Wässern zu kleben!" — Das Kind war neugierig zu wissen, wer sie denn eigentlich seyen, da sie so schön leuchteten und doch gar so mißmuthig schienen. — Da begann das zweite zu berichten, wie es auch einmal ein Kind gewesen und dann groß geworden sey; wie es aber frühzeitig seinen einzigen Spaß daran gehabt, den Leuten etwas weiß zu machen, um recht vornehm und gelehrt zu scheinen. Immer habe es einen ganzen Strom glatter Worte über die Leute ausgeschüttet, und so allmählig einen schimmernden Dunst um sich her verbreitet, daß die Leute, wie die Fliegen, darnach hingeflattert seyen, bis sie endlich darin untergegangen. Da sey aber einmal ein schlichter Mann in seine Nähe gekommen, der habe nur ein paar einfältige Worte gesprochen, und plötzlich sey der Dunst zerstoben und zerflogen, daß es ganz nackt und bloß mit seinem aufgedunsenen Leib — aller Welt zum Spotte da gestanden habe. Der schlichte Mann aber habe sich mitleidig von ihm abgewendet, während es in Schaam und Aerger vergangen sey, und als es wieder zu sich gekommen, da habe es sich wollen hinaufschwingen, weil es gehofft, da drüben ein besseres Schicksal zu finden. Aber seine Flügel seyen ganz durchnäßt gewesen und immer dunkler sey es ihm vor den Augen geworden. Da habe es sich Anfangs gar nicht mehr wiederfinden können, bis es endlich an einem Sumpfe sich als Irrlicht erkannt und nun nicht mehr weiter habe kommen können. —

"Mir ist es ganz anders ergangen," sprach das erste — "ich war zwar auch unter Leuten, aber statt daß ich jetzt leuchte ohne zu wärmen, brannte ich damals ohne zu leuchten. Schon, als ich noch Kind war, schenkten die Leute mich immer mir selber ein, so daß ich früh von mir selbst betrunken war. Sah ich dann jemand leuchten, dann hätte ich sein Licht ausblasen mögen, und je mehr ich das wollte, destomehr zog das bischen, Licht, das ich um mich hatte, sich in mein Allerinnerstes zurück, und brannte hier ingrimmig, während ich nach außen immer dunkler wurde. Wollte aber einer, der da leuchtete, mir liebreich von seinem Lichte schenken, dann brach von innen meine Flamme hervor, um das Licht zu vernichten. Aber das Licht ließ die Flamme ungestört durch sich hinschießen, und leuchtete nur noch heller, während ich schier ausgebrannt war. So begegnete mir einmal ein kleines Kind, das vor sich hinlächelnd mit einem Kreuze von Palmstäbchen spielte und einen strahlenden Ring auf den goldenen Locken trug. Es faßte mich freundlich bei der Hand, schaute mit seinen himmelblauen Augen mich an, und sprach: "Sieh, lieber Mann, du bist zwar noch sehr dunkel und trübe; willst du aber wieder ein Kind seyn, wie ich bin, dann sollst du auch einen Strahlenring haben, wie ich." — Als ich das hörte, ärgerte ich mich so über mich selbst und das Kind, daß mich das Feuer verzehrte. Nun wollte ich hinauf in die Sonne, um mir dort Strahlen zu holen, aber unterwegs stießen mich ihre Strahlen wieder mit den Worten herab: "Gehe du nur wieder hin, wo du hergekommen bist, du finsteres Zornfeuer; denn die Sonne leuchtet nur in Liebe, und nur die begierliche Erde verkehrt ihr mildes Licht zuweilen in heißen Brand; darum fliehe zurück, denn nur bei deines Gleichen darfst du wohnen." Ich schütterte zusammen, und als ich mich wieder aufraffte, stand ich wie eine Fackeldistel, mit schimmerndem, aber kaltem Kopfe am stillen Gewässer." Das Kind war über den Erzählungen eingeschlafen; denn es wußte Nichts von der Welt und den Menschen, und wußte daher auch nicht, was es aus jenen Erzählungen machen sollte. Die Müdigkeit hatte aber ein deutlicheres Wort zu ihm gesprochen; das hatte es verstanden und war eingeschlafen.

XII.

UND ES SCHLIEF sanft und es schlief fest, bis das Morgenroth sich auf die Berge stellte, und die Ankunft seiner Herrin, der Sonne, verkündigte. Denn als die Verkündigung sich über die Flur und den Wald ergoß, da erwachte ein tausendstimmiges Echo, und es war an kein Schlafen mehr zu denken. Als aber gar die königliche Sonnenjungfrau selbst sich erhob, und zuerst ihr Diadem über den Bergen heraufblitzte, bis sie selbst in ihrem vollen Glanze, geschmückt mit allen Reizen der ewigen Jugend, strahlend und herrlich dastand, und ihr liebender Blick segnend alle irdischen Geschöpfe umfaßte, vom stolzen, gewaltigen Eichenbaum an bis zum niedergetretenen Grashalm, — da erscholl ihr aus allen Brüsten, aus allen Kehlen ein jubelvoller Preisgesang, und es war auf der Flur wie im Walde, als sey die ganze Natur zu einer Kirche geworden, deren Wölbung der Himmel, deren Altar die Berge, und alle Creaturen die Gemeinde und die Sonne der Priester oder das Allerheiligste oder das Auge Gottes waren. — Aber das Kind trat heraus und war froh, weil die Vöglein so feierlich sangen und alles ihm in Himmels=Wonne und in Lebenslust zu hüpfen und zu tanzen schien. Hier flogen zwei Finklein durch das Gebüsch und suchten zwitschernd sich einander zu erhaschen; dort sprangen Knospen von einander und ein Paar Blättlein kamen heraus und legten sich breit in die Sonne, als wenn sie nimmer wieder weg wollten; hier zitterte äugelnd und blinkend ein Thautropfen an einer Grasspitze und wußte nicht, daß schon unter ihm ein Möslein nach ihm dürstete; dort schwärmten Fliegen in die Höhen, als wollten sie weit über den Wald hinaus, — und so war überall Bewegung und Leben und das Kind hatte seine herzige Freude daran. Es setzte sich hin auf ein kleines Rasenplätzchen, über welches ein Nußstrauch sich wölbte, und dachte nun seine Freude so recht tropfenweis zu schlürfen. Zuerst entfernte es noch einige Brombeerranken, die in der Nähe ihm mit ihren scharfen Stachelhaken drohten; dann bog es einige Aeste, die ihm die Aussicht zu sehr verdeckten. Drauf schob es einige Steine weg, damit es seine Füße bequem aufstellen konnte; und als es auch hiermit fertig war, besann es sich, was noch zu thun wäre, und als es nichts fand, stand es auf, um seine bekannte Libelle zu suchen, und sie zu bitten, es doch wieder aus dem Walde in's Freie zu führen. Auf halbem Wege begegnete sie ihm, und entschuldigte sich, daß sie aus Ermüdung sich heute verschlafen habe. Das Kind dachte nicht an die Vergangenheit, und wäre sie auch der vorletzte Augenblick gewesen, sondern wünschte jetzt nur, wieder hinaus aus dem engen Walde zu kommen, indem seine Brust hoch aufschlug und es vermeinte, draußen freiern Athem schöpfen zu können. Die Libelle zeigte ihm, voranfliegend, den Weg bis an die letzten Hecken des Waldes, von wo aus das Kind sein Hüttchen in der Ferne wahrnehmen konnte, und flog dann zu den Seinigen zurück.

XIII.

Das Kind trat hinaus auf das frisch bethaute Ackerfeld, von dem tausend kleine Sonnen ihm entgegenblitzten und eine Lerche sich wirbelnd emporhob. Die Lerche aber verkündigte die Freuden des kommenden Jahres, und erregte unendliche Erwartungen, dieweil sie sich kreisend immer höher schwang, bis ihr Gesang endlich dem leisen Gelispel eines Engels zu vergleichen war, der im reinen Himmelblau mit dem Frühling selige Zwiesprache hielt. Das Kind hatte das erdfarbene Vöglein sich emporschwingen gesehen, und es kam ihm nun vor, als habe die Erde es aus ihrem Schooße entlassen, um der Sonne ihren Jubel und ihren Dank darob zu verkündigen, daß sie ihr wieder das strahlende Antlitz in Liebe und Freundlichkeit zugewendet. Die Lerche aber wirbelte über den hoffnungsvollen Fluren ein fröhliches und helljauchzendes Lied, und sang von der Lieblichkeit des Morgenrothes, und dem jugendfrischen Spiele der ersten Sonnenstrahlen, von dem lustigen Hervorspringen der Blumen und dem freudigen Aufschießen der Fruchthalme, und das gefiel dem Kinde über die Maßen wohl. Aber sie schwang sich in ihren Kreisen immer höher, und linder und leiser ertönte ihr Lied, und sie sang von der ersten Wonne der Geliebten und ihrem tändelnden Kosen und Necken, von Lustwandeln an Freundeshand auf sonnigen, freien Bergeshöhen, und von froher Erwartung aus blauer, duftiger Ferne. Das Kind verstand nicht recht, was es hörte, und hätte doch gerne verstanden; denn es meinte nun selbst in Erwartung wunderherrlicher Dinge zu seyn. Scharf sah es dem unermüdlichen Vöglein nach in die Höhe; aber das war verschwunden im Dufte des Frühlings. Da wandte das Kind sein Köpflein mit einer Seite nach oben, um zu lauschen, ob der kleine Frühlingsbote gar nicht mehr singe. Da vernahm es in verschwimmenden Tönen, wie es sang von der Sehnsucht nach dem heiteren Elemente der Freiheit, nach dem reinen allgegenwärtigen Lichte, — von den seligen Vorgefühlen der ersehnten Befreiung und von dem Ueberfließen in das Meer der göttlichen Wonne. — Noch lange horchte das Kind; denn die Töne des Gesanges trugen es hin, wo seine Gedanken noch nicht hinreichten, und es fühlte sich glücklicher als je in diesem leichten Emporfluge. Aber die Lerche kam jetzt rasch wieder herab, dieweil ihr Körperchen noch zu schwer war für den flüchtigen Aether, und ihre Flügel nicht stark und nicht groß genug gewesen für das reine Element. —

Da lachten die rothen Kornblumen das unscheinbare Vöglein aus, und schrien einander und den ringsumherstehenden Fruchthalmen mit greller Stimme zu: "Nun seht ihr's ja, daß es nichts ist mit dem Hoch-fliegen, und dem Streben nach der leeren Luft; da verliert man seine Zeit und bringt nichts als müde Glieder und einen leeren Magen mit zurück. Da wollte das gemeine, schlechtgekleidete Thierchen sich über uns erheben und führte einen gewaltigen Lärm. Dafür liegt es nun auch am Boden und kann kaum mehr Athem schöpfen. Wir aber haben hübsch Fuß beim Mahl gehalten, und sind verständigerweise bei der Wirklichkeit geblieben, und während der Zeit um ein Schönes dicker und größer geworden." Laut klatschten die anderen kleinen Rothmäntel ihm Beifall, daß dem Kinde die Ohren davon gellten, und es sie wegen ihrer hämischen Schadenfreude eben züchtigen wollte, als eine frisch aufgeblühte, himmelblaue Cyane mit sanfter Stimme das Wort nahm, und also zu ihren jüngeren Gespielinnen sprach: "Laßt euch, ihr Lieben, nicht irre führen durch den Schein, und die Rede, die nur auf dem Scheine beruht. Wohl ist die Lerche ermüdet, und die Räume sind leer, in welche die Lerche sich aufgeschwungen; aber nicht das Leere ist es, was die Lerche gesucht hat und nicht leer ist die Suchende zurückgekommen. Nach dem Lichte und nach der Freiheit hat sie gestrebt, und das Licht und die Freiheit hat sie gepriesen. Die Erde und ihre Genüsse hat sie verlassen, dafür aber hat sie auch reine Lebensluft getrunken, und hat gesehen, daß nicht die Erde, sondern daß die Sonne das Feststehende sey. Und wenn auch die Erde sie wieder herabgefordert hat, dann kann die Erde doch nur das *Erdige* an ihr festhalten. Das *Singende* aber und das *Auffliegende* in ihr gehört schon der Sonne an, und wird dort eingehen in das Licht und die Freiheit, wenn die blöden Prahler schon längst wieder in das dunkle Gefängniß der Erde werden hinabgezogen und begraben seyn." Und die Lerche vernahm die wohlwollende Rede, und neu gekräftigt schwang sie von Neuem sich hinauf in die heitere Bläue. Das Kind aber klatschte in die Händchen vor Freude, daß das Vöglein wieder aufgeflogen war, und die Kornblumen verstummten und vor Schaam entfärbten sich ihre rothen Gesichter.

XIV.

UND DAS KIND war wieder recht fröhlich geworden, und athmete wieder frei, und dachte nicht mehr daran, in sein Hüttchen zurückzukehren. Ging doch nichts von Allem, was es sah, zurück; vielmehr zog und strebte Alles hinaus, oder hinauf — in's Freie; die rosigen Apfelblüthen aus der engen Knospe, wie die wirbelnden Lerchentöne aus dem engen Brüstlein. Die Keime sprengten die Flügelthüren des Saamens, und durchbrachen die Dämme der Erde, um an's Licht zu kommen; die Gräser zerrissen ihre Bande und eilten als Halme in die Höhe. Selbst die Felsen waren weich geworden, und ließen kleine Flechten und Möslein ausgehen, zum Zeichen, daß auch sie nicht ewig verschlossen bleiben wollten. Und die Blumen schickten Farben und Düfte aus in alle Welt, weil sie ihr Bestes nicht für sich behalten, sondern das Echo seyn wollten der Sonne und der Sterne, die auch ihre Wärme und ihre Strahlen hinaussendeten in den Frühling. Aber auch manches Mücklein und Käferlein zerschellte das drückende Wiegengrab, in dem es eingesperrt lag, und kroch langsam und noch halbbetäubt aus der Hülle, entfaltete und schüttelte die zarten Flüglein, versuchte sie zu schlagen, und war schon gestärkt, und that einen Flug in das Weite. Und wie die Schmetterlinge sich prangend aus der Puppe emporschwangen, so machte jede eingewinterte und verhüllte Sehnsucht und Hoffnung sich frei und schiffte mit vollen Segeln hinaus in das laue und blaue und offene und fluthende Meer des Frühlings.

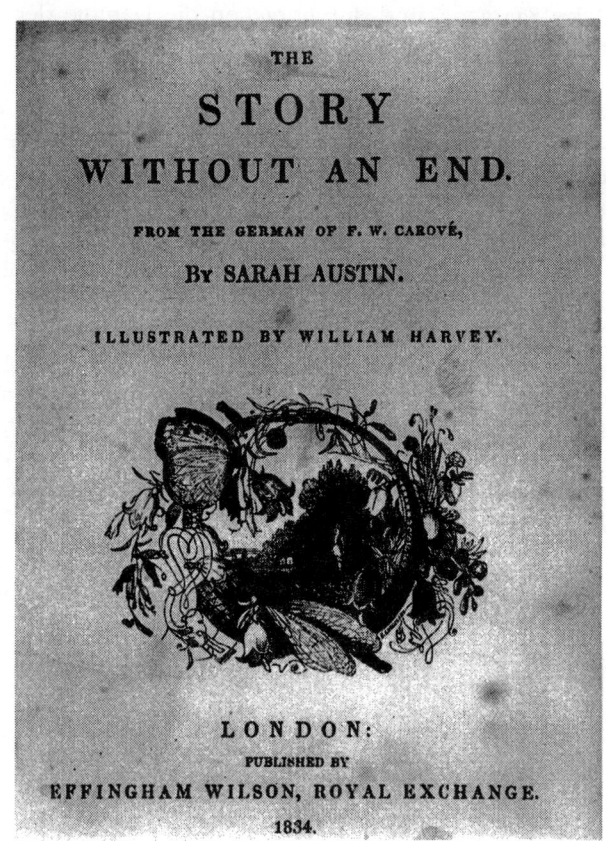

Titlepage of the first edition of The Story Without an End

Sarah Austin

The Story Without an End

TO MY DAUGHTER.

My Dear Child,

The story you love so much in German, I dedicate to you in English. It was in compliance with your earnest wish that other children might share the delight it has so often afforded you, that I translated it; so that it is, in some sort, yours of right. Let us hope that your confident expectations of sympathy in your pleasure may not be disappointed; or that, if others think the story less beautiful that you do, they may find compensation in the graceful designs it has inspired.

You have often regretted that it left off so soon, and would, I believe, "have been glad to hear more and more, and for ever." The continuation you have longed for lies in a wide and magnificent book, which contains more wonderful and glorious things than all our favourite fairy-tales put together. But to read in that book, so as to discover all its beautiful meanings, you must have pure, clear eyes, and a humble, loving heart; otherwise you will complain, as some do, that it is dim and puzzling; or, as others, that it is dull and monotonous.

May you continue to read in it with new curiosity, new delight, and new profit; and to find it, as long as you live, the untiring "Story without an End."

Your affectionate Mother,
S. A.

London
Nov. 16th, 1833.

I.

THERE WAS ONCE a Child who lived in a little hut, and in the hut there was nothing but a little bed and a looking-glass which hung in a dark corner. Now the Child cared nothing at all about the looking-glass; but as soon as the first sunbeam glided softly through the casement and kissed his sweet eyelids, and the finch and the linnet waked him merrily with their morning songs, he arose, and went out into the green meadow. And he begged flour of the primrose, and sugar of the violet, and butter of the butter-cup; he shook dew-drops from the cowslip into the cup of a hare-bell; spread out a large lime leaf, set his little breakfast upon it, and feasted daintily. Sometimes he invited a humming bee, oftener a gay butterfly, to partake his feast; but his favourite guest was the blue dragonfly. The bee murmured a great deal, in a solemn tone, about his riches: but the Child thought that if *he* were a bee heaps of treasure would not make him gay and happy; and that it must be much more delightful and glorious to float about in the free and fresh breezes of spring, and to hum joyously in the web of the sunbeams, than, with heavy feet and heavy heart, to stow the silver wax and the golden honey into cells.

To this the butterfly assented; and he told, how, once on a time, he too had been greedy and sordid; how he had thought of nothing but eating, and had never once turned his eyes upwards to the blue heavens. At length, however, a complete change had come over him; and instead of crawling spiritless about the dirty earth, half dreaming, he all at once awaked as out of a deep sleep. And now he would rise into the air; — and it was his greatest joy sometimes to play with the light, and to reflect the heavens in the bright eyes of his wings; sometimes to listen to the soft language of the flowers and catch their secrets. Such talk delighted the Child, and his breakfast was the sweeter to him, and the sunshine on leaf and flower seemed to him more bright and cheering.

But when the bee had flown off to beg from flower to flower, and the butterfly had fluttered away to his play-fellows, the dragonfly still remained, poised on a blade of grass. Her slender and burnished body, more brightly and deeply blue than the deep blue sky, glistened in the sunbeam; and her netlike wings laughed at the flowers because *they* could not fly, but must stand still and abide the wind and the rain. The dragonfly sipped a little of the Child's clear dew-drops and blue violet-honey, and then whispered her winged words. And the Child made an end of his repast, closed his dark blue eyes, bent down his beautiful head, and listened to the sweet prattle.

Then the dragonfly told much of the merry life in the green wood; how sometimes she played hide-and-seek with her playfellows under the broad leaves of the oak and the beech trees; or hunt-the-hare along the surface of the still waters; sometimes quietly watched the sunbeams, as they flew busily from moss to flower and from flower to bush, and shed life and warmth over all. But at night, she said, the moonbeams glided softly around the wood, and dropped dew into the mouths of all the thirsty plants; and when the dawn pelted the slumberers with the soft roses of heaven, some of the half drunken flowers looked up and smiled; but most of them could not so much as raise their heads for a long, long time.

Such stories did the dragonfly tell; and as the Child sat motionless with his eyes shut, and his head rested on his little hand, she thought he had fallen asleep; — so she poised her double wings and flew into the rustling wood.

II.

But the child was only sunk into a dream of delight, and was wishing *he* were a sunbeam or a moonbeam; and he would have been glad to hear more and more, and for ever. But at last, as all was still, he opened his eyes and looked around for his dear guest; but she was flown far away; so he could not bear to sit there any longer alone, and he rose and went to the gurgling brook. It gushed and rolled so merrily, and tumbled so wildly along as it hurried to throw itself head-over-heels into the river, just as if the great, massy rock out of which it sprang, were close behind it, and could only be escaped by a break-neck leap.

Then the Child began to talk to the little waves, and asked them whence they came. They would not stay to give him an answer, but danced away, one over another; till at last, that the sweet Child might not be grieved, a drop of water stopped behind a piece of rock. From her the Child heard strange histories, but he could not understand them all, for she told him about her former life, and about the depths of the mountain.

"A long while ago," said the drop of water, "I lived with my countless sisters in the great ocean, in peace and unity. We had all sorts of pastimes; sometimes we mounted up high into the air, and peeped at the stars; then we sank plump down deep below, and looked how the coral builders work till they are tired, that they may reach the light of day at last. But I was conceited, and thought myself much better than my sisters. And so one day when the sun rose out of the sea, I clung fast to one of his hot beams, and thought that now I should reach the stars, and become one of them. But I had not ascended far, when the sunbeam shook me off, and in spite of all I could say or do, let me fall into a dark cloud. And soon a flash of fire darted through the cloud, and now I thought I must surely die; but the whole cloud laid itself down softly upon the top of a mountain, and so I escaped with my fright, and a black eye. Now I thought I should remain hidden, when, all on a sudden, I slipped over a round pebble, fell from one stone to another, down into the depths of the mountain, till at last it was pitch dark, and I could neither see nor hear any thing. Then I found, indeed, that 'pride goeth before a fall,' resigned myself to my fate, and, as I had already laid aside all my unhappy pride in the cloud, my portion was now the salt of humility; and after undergoing many purifications from the hidden virtues of metals and minerals, I was at length permitted to come up once more into the free cheerful air; and now will I run back to my sisters, and there wait patiently till I am called to something better."

But hardly had she done, when the root of a forget-me-not caught the drop of water by her hair and sucked her in, that she might become a floweret, and twinkle brightly as a blue star on the green firmament of earth.

III.

The Child did not very well know what to think of all this; he went thoughtfully home and laid himself on his little bed; and all night long he was wandering about on the ocean, and among the stars, and over the dark mountain. But the moon loved to look on the slumbering Child as he lay with his little head softly pillowed on his right arm. She lingered a long time before his little window, and went slowly away to lighten the dark chamber of some sick person.

As the moon's soft light lay on the Child's eyelids, he fancied he sat in a golden boat, on a great, great water; countless stars swam glittering on the dark mirror. He stretched out his hand to catch the nearest star, but it had vanished, and the water sprayed up against him. Then he saw clearly that these were not the real stars; he looked up to heaven, and wished he could fly thither.

But in the mean time the moon had wandered on her way; and now the Child was led in his dream into the clouds, and he thought he was sitting on a white sheep, and he saw many lambs grazing around him. He tried to catch a little lamb to play with, but it was all mist and vapour; and the Child was sorrowful, and wished himself down again in his own meadow, where his own lamb was sporting gaily about.

Meanwhile the moon was gone to sleep behind the mountains, and all around was dark. Then the Child dreamt that he fell down into the dark, gloomy caverns of the mountain, and at that he was so frightened, that he suddenly awoke, just as morning opened her clear eye over the nearest hill.

IV.

THE CHILD STARTED up, and, to recover himself from his fright, went into the little flower-garden behind his cottage, where the beds were surrounded by ancient palm-trees, and where he knew that all the flowers would nod kindly at him. But behold, the tulip turned up her nose, and the ranunculus held her head as stiffly as possible, that she might not bow good-morrow to him. The rose, with her fair round cheeks, smiled and greeted the Child lovingly; so he went up to her and kissed her fragrant mouth. And then the rose tenderly complained that he so seldom came into the garden, and that she gave out her bloom and her fragrance the live-long day in vain; for the other flowers either could not see her, because they were too low, or did not care to look at her, because they themselves were so rich in bloom and fragrance. But she was most delighted when she glowed in the blooming head of a child, and could pour out all her heart's secrets to him in sweet odours. Among other things, the rose whispered in his ear that she was the Fulness of Beauty.

And in truth the Child, while looking at her beauty, seemed to have quite forgotten to go on; till the blue larkspur called to him, and asked whether he cared nothing more about his faithful friend; she said that she was unchanged, and that even in death she should look upon him with eyes of unfading blue.

The Child thanked her for her true-heartedness, and passed on to the hyacinth who stood near the puffy, full-cheeked, gaudy tulips. Even from a distance the hyacinth sent forth kisses to him, for she knew not how to express her love. Although she was not remarkable for her beauty, yet the Child felt himself wondrously attracted by her, for he thought no flower loved him so well. But the hyacinth poured out her full heart and wept bitterly, because she stood so lonely; the tulips indeed were her countrymen, but they were so cold and unfeeling that she was ashamed of them. The Child encouraged her, and told her he did not think things were so bad as she fancied. The tulips spoke their love in bright looks, while she uttered her's in fragrant words; that these, indeed, were lovelier and more intelligible, but that the others were not to be despised.

Then the hyacinth was comforted, and said she would be content; and the Child went on to the powdered auricula, who, in her bashfulness, looked kindly up to him, and would gladly have given him more than kind looks, had she had more to give. But the Child was satisfied with her modest greeting; he felt that he was poor too, and he saw the deep, thoughtful colours that lay beneath her golden dust. But the humble flower of her own accord sent him to her neighbour, the lily, whom she willingly acknowledged as her queen. And when the Child came to the lily, the slender flower waved to and fro, and bowed her pale head with gentle pride and stately modesty, and sent forth a fragrant greeting to him. The Child knew not what had come to him: it reached his inmost heart, so that his eyes filled with soft tears. Then he marked how the lily gazed with a clear and steadfast eye upon the sun, and how the sun looked down again into her pure chalice, and how, amid this interchange of looks, the three golden threads united in the centre. And the Child heard how one scarlet lady-bird at the bottom of the cup, said to another, "knowest thou not that we dwell in the flower of heaven?" and the other replied, "yes, and now will the mystery be fulfilled." And as the Child saw and heard all this, the dim image of his unknown parents, as it were veiled in a holy light, floated before his eyes: he strove to grasp it, but the light was gone, and the Child slipped, and would have fallen, had not the branch of a currant bush* caught and held him; and he took some of the bright berries for his morning's meal, and went back to his hut and stripped the little branches.

---

* The red currant is called in Germany, *Johannis-beere*, St. John's berry.

V.

But in the hut he staid not long, all was so gloomy, close, and silent within; and abroad every thing seemed to smile, and to exult in the clear and unbounded space. Therefore the Child went out into the green wood, of which the dragonfly had told him such pleasant stories. But he found every thing far more beautiful and lovely even than she had described it; for all about, where-ever he went, the tender moss pressed his little feet, and the delicate grass embraced his knees, and the flowers kissed his hands, and even the branches stroked his cheeks with a kind and refreshing touch, and the high trees threw their fragrant shade around him.

There was no end to his delight. The little birds warbled and sang, and fluttered and hopped about, and the delicate wood-flowers gave out their beauty and their odours; and every sweet sound took a sweet odour by the hand, and thus walked through the open door of the Child's heart, and held a joyous nuptial dance therein. But the nightingale and the lily of the valley led the dance; for the nightingale sang of nought but love, and the lily breathed of nought but innocence, and he was the bridegroom and she was the bride. And the nightingale was never weary of repeating the same thing a hundred times over, for the spring of love which gushed from his heart was ever new; and the lily bowed her head bashfully, that no one might see her glowing heart. And yet the one lived so solely and entirely in the other, that no one could see whether the notes of the nightingale were floating lilies, or the lilies visible notes, falling like dew-drops from the nightingale's throat.

The child's heart was full of joy even to the brim. He set himself down, and he almost thought he should like to take root there, and live for ever among the sweet plants and flowers, and so become a true sharer in all their gentle pleasures. For he felt a deep delight in the still, secluded, twilight existence of the mosses and small herbs, which felt not the storm nor the frost, nor the scorching sunbeam; but dwelt quietly among their many friends and neighbours, feasting in peace and good fellowship on the dew and the cool shadows which the mighty trees shed upon them. To them it was a high festival when a sunbeam chanced to visit their lowly home; whilst the tops of the lofty trees could find joy and beauty only in the purple rays of morning or evening.

VI.

AND AS THE Child sat there, a little mouse rustled from among the dry leaves of the former year, and a lizard half glided from a crevice in the rock, and both of them fixed their bright eyes upon the little stranger; and when they saw that he designed them no evil, they took courage and came nearer to him.

"I should like to live with you," said the Child to the two little creatures, in a soft subdued voice, that he might not frighten them. "Your chambers are so snug, so warm, and yet so shaded, and the flowers grow in at your windows, and the birds sing you their morning song, and call you to table and to bed with their clear warblings."

"Yes," said the mouse, "it would be all very well if all the plants bore nuts and mast, instead of those silly flowers; and if I were not obliged to grub under ground in the spring, and gnaw the bitter roots, whilst they are dressing themselves in their fine flowers and flaunting it to the world, as if they had endless stores of honey in their cellars."

"Hold your tongue," interrupted the lizard pertly, "do you think, because you are grey, that other people must throw away their handsome clothes, or let them lie in the dark wardrobe under ground, and wear nothing but grey too? I am not so envious. The flowers may dress themselves as they like for me; they pay for it out of their own pockets, and they feed bees and beetles from their cups; but what I want to know is, of what use are birds in the world? Such a fluttering and chattering, truly, from morning early to evening late, that one is worried and stunned to death, and there is never a day's peace for them. And they do nothing; only snap up the flies and the spiders out of the mouths of such as I. For my part, I should be perfectly satisfied, provided all the birds in the world were flies and beetles."

The Child changed colour, and his heart was sick and saddened when he heard their evil tongues. He could not imagine how any body could speak ill of the beautiful flowers, or scoff at his beloved birds. He was waked out of a sweet dream, and the wood seemed to him lonely and desert, and he was ill at ease. He started up hastily, so that the mouse and the lizard shrank back alarmed, and did not look around them till they thought themselves safe out of the reach of the stranger with the large, severe eyes.

VII.

But the Child went away from the place; and as he hung down his head thoughtfully, he did not observe that he took the wrong path, nor see how the flowers on either side bowed their heads to welcome him, nor hear how the old birds from the boughs, and the young from the nests, cried aloud to him, "God bless thee, our dear little prince." And he went on and on, farther and farther, into the deep wood; and he thought over the foolish and heartless talk of the two selfish chatterers, and could not understand it. He would fain have forgotten it, but he could not. And the more he pondered, the more it seemed to him as if a malicious spider had spun her web around him, and as if his eyes were weary with trying to look through it.

And suddenly he came to a still water, above which young beeches lovingly entwined their arms. He looked in the water, and his eyes were riveted to it as if by enchantment. He could not move, but stood and gazed in the soft, placid mirror, from the bosom of which the tender green foliage, with the deep blue heavens between, gleamed so wondrously upon him. His sorrow was all forgotten, and even the echo of the discord in his little heart was hushed. That heart was once more in his eyes; and fain would he have drunk in the soft beauty of the colours that lay beneath him, or have plunged into the lovely deep.

Then the breeze began to sigh among the tree-tops. The Child raised his eyes and saw overhead the quivering green, and the deep blue behind it, and he knew not whether he were waking or dreaming: which were the real leaves and the real heaven, — those in the depths above, or in the depths beneath? Long did the Child waver, and his thoughts floated in a delicious dreaminess from one to the other, till the dragonfly flew to him in affectionate haste, and with rustling wings greeted her kind host. The Child returned her greeting, and was glad to meet an acquaintance with whom he could share the rich feast of his joy. But first he asked the dragonfly if she could decide for him between the Upper and the Nether — the heighth and the depth? The dragonfly flew above, and beneath, and around; but the water spake: "The foliage and the sky above are not the true ones: the leaves wither and fall; the sky is often overcast, and sometimes quite dark." Then the leaves and the sky said, "The water only apes us; it must change its pictures at our pleasure, and can retain none." Then the dragonfly remarked, that the heighth and the depth existed only in the eyes of the Child, and that the leaves and the sky were true and real only in his thoughts; because in the mind alone the picture was permanent and enduring, and could be carried with him whithersoever he went.

This she said to the Child; but she immediately warned him to return, for the leaves were already beating the tattoo in the evening breeze, and the lights were disappearing one by one in every corner. Then the Child confessed to her with alarm that he knew not how he should find the way back, and that he feared the dark night would overtake him if he attempted to go home alone; so the dragonfly flew on before him, and shewed him a cave in the rock where he might pass the night. And the Child was well content; for he had often wished to try if he could sleep out of his accustomed bed.

VIII.

BUT THE DRAGONFLY was fleet, and gratitude strengthened her wings to pay her host the honour she owed him. And truly in the dim twilight good counsel and guidance were scarce. She flitted hither and thither without knowing rightly what was to be done; when, by the last vanishing sunbeam, she saw hanging on the edge of the cave some strawberries who had drunk so deep of the evening-red, that their heads were quite heavy. Then she flew up to a harebell who stood near, and whispered in her ear that the lord and king of all the flowers was in the wood, and ought to be received and welcomed as beseemed his dignity. Aglaia did not need that this should be repeated. She began to ring her sweet bells with all her might; and when her neighbour heard the sound, she rang hers also; and soon all the harebells, great and small, were in motion, and rang as if it had been for the nuptials of their mother earth herself, with the prince of the sun. The tone of the blue bells was deep and rich, and that of the white, high and clear, and all blended together in a delicious harmony.

But the birds were fast asleep in their high nests, and the ears of the other animals were not delicate enough, or were too much overgrown with hair, to hear them. The fireflies alone heard the joyous peal, for they were akin to the flowers, through their common ancestor, light. They inquired of their nearest relation, the lily of the valley, and from her they heard that a large flower had just passed along the footpath more blooming than the loveliest rose, and with two stars more brilliant than those of the brightest firefly, and that it must needs be their king. Then all the fireflies flew up and down the foot path, and sought every where, till at length they came, as the dragonfly had hoped they would, to the cave.

And now, as they looked at the Child, and every one of them saw itself reflected in his clear eyes, they rejoiced exceedingly, and called all their fellows together, and alighted on the bushes all around; and soon it was so light in the cave, that herb and grass began to grow as if it had been broad day. Now, indeed, was the joy and triumph of the dragonfly complete. The Child was delighted with the merry and silvery tones of the bells, and with the many little bright-eyed companions around him, and with the deep red strawberries which bowed down their head to his touch.

IX.

And when he had eaten his fill, he sat down on the soft moss, crossed one little leg over the other, and began to gossip with the fireflies. And as he so often thought on his unknown parents, he asked them who were their parents. Then the one nearest to him gave him answer; and he told how that they were formerly flowers, but none of those who thrust their rooty hands greedily into the ground and draw nourishment from the dingy earth, only to make themselves fat and large withal; but that the light was dearer to them than any thing, even at night; and while the other flowers slept, they gazed unwearied on the light, and drank it in with eager adoration, — sun and moon and star light. And the light had so thoroughly purified them, that they had not sucked in poisonous juices like the yellow flowers of the earth, but sweet odours for sick and fainting hearts, and oil of potent, ethereal virtue for the weak and the wounded; and, at length, when their autumn came, they did not, like the others, wither and sink down, leaf and flower, to be swallowed up by the darksome earth, but shook off their earthly garment and mounted aloft into the clear air. But there it was so wondrously bright, that sight failed them; and when they came to themselves again, they were fireflies, each sitting on a withered flower-stalk.

And now the Child liked the bright-eyed flies better than ever; and he talked a little longer with them, and inquired why they shewed themselves so much more in spring. They did it, they said, in the hope that their gold-green radiance might allure their cousins, the flowers, to the pure love of light.

X.

DURING THIS CONVERSATION the dragonfly had been preparing a bed for her host. The moss upon which the Child sat had grown a foot high behind his back, out of pure joy; but the dragonfly and her sisters had so revelled upon it, that it was now laid at its length along the cave. The dragonfly had awakened every spider in the neighbourhood out of her sleep, and when they saw the brilliant light, they had set to work spinning so industriously that their web hung down like a curtain before the mouth of the cave. But as the Child saw the ant peeping up at him, he entreated the fireflies not to deprive themselves any longer of their merry games in the wood, on his account. And the dragonfly and her sisters raised the curtain till the Child had laid him down to rest, and then let it fall again, that the mischievous gnats might not get in to disturb his slumbers.

The Child laid himself down to sleep, for he was very tired; but he could not sleep, for his couch of moss was quite another thing than his little bed, and the cave was all strange to him. He turned himself on one side and then on the other, and as nothing would do, he raised himself and sat upright to wait till sleep might choose to come. But sleep would not come at all; — and the only wakeful eyes in the whole wood were the Child's. For the harebells had rung themselves weary, and the fireflies had flown about till they were tired, and even the dragonfly, who would fain have kept watch in front of the cave, had dropped sound asleep.

The wood grew stiller and stiller: here and there fell a dry leaf which had been driven from its old dwelling place by a fresh one; here and there a young bird gave a soft chirp when its mother squeezed it in the nest; — and from time to time a gnat hummed for a minute or two in the curtain, till a spider crept on tip-toe along its web, and gave him such a gripe in the wind-pipe as soon spoiled his trumpeting.

And the deeper the silence became, the more intently did the Child listen, and at last the slightest sound thrilled him from head to foot. At length, all was still as death in the wood; and the world seemed as if it never would wake again. The Child bent forward to see whether it were as dark abroad as in the cave, but he saw nothing save the pitch dark night, who had wrapped every thing in her thick veil. Yet as he looked upwards his eyes met the friendly glance of two or three stars, and this was a most joyful surprise to him, for he felt himself no longer so entirely alone. The stars were, indeed, far, far away, but yet he knew them, and they knew him; for they looked into his eyes.

The Child's whole soul was fixed in his gaze; and it seemed to him as if he must needs fly out of the darksome cave, thither where the stars were beaming with such pure and serene light; and he felt how poor and lowly he was, when he thought of their brilliancy; and how cramped and fettered, when he thought of their free, unbounded course along the heavens.

XI.

But the stars went on their course, and left their glittering picture only a little while before the Child's eyes. Even this faded, and then vanished quite away. And he was beginning to feel tired, and to wish to lay himself down again, when a flickering will-o'-the-wisp appeared from behind a bush, — so that the Child thought, at first, one of the stars had wandered out of its way and had come to visit him, and to take him with it. And the Child breathed quick with joy and surprise, and then the will-o'-the'-wisp came nearer and set himself down on a damp, mossy stone in front of the cave, and another fluttered quickly after him, and sat down over against him and sighed deeply, "Thank God, then, that I can rest at last!"

"Yes," said the other, "for that you may thank the innocent Child who sleeps there within; it was his pure breath that freed us." — "Are you then," said the Child, hesitatingly, "not of yon stars which wander so brightly there above?" — "Oh, if we were stars," replied the first, "we should pursue our tranquil path through the pure element, and should leave this wood and the whole darksome earth to itself." — "And not," said the other, "sit brooding on the face of the shallow pool."

The Child was curious to know who these could be who shone so beautifully, and yet seemed so discontented. Then the first began to relate how he had been a child too, and how, as he grew up, it had always been his greatest delight to deceive people and play them tricks, to show his wit and cleverness. He had always, he said, poured such a stream of smooth words over people, and encompassed himself with such a shining mist, that men had been attracted by it to their own hurt. But once on a time there appeared a plain man who only spoke two or three simple words, and suddenly the bright mist vanished, and left him naked and deformed, to the scorn and mockery of the whole world. But the man had turned away his face from him in pity, while he was almost dead with shame and anger. And when he came to himself again, he knew not what had befallen him till, at length, he found that it was his fate to hover, without rest or change, over the surface of the bog as a will-o'-the-wisp.

"With me it fell out quite otherwise," said the first: "Instead of giving light without warmth, as I now do, I burned without shining. When I was only a child, people gave way to me in every thing, so that I was intoxicated with self-love. If I saw any one shine, I longed to put out his light; and the more intensely I wished this, the more did my own small glimmering turn back upon myself, and inwardly burn fiercely, while all without was darker than ever. But if any one who shone more brightly would have kindly given me of his light, then did my inward flame burst forth to destroy him. But the flame passed through the light and harmed it not; it shone only the more brightly, while I was withered and exhausted. And once upon a time I met a little smiling child, who played with a cross of palm branches, and wore a beamy coronet around his golden locks. He took me kindly by the hand and said, 'My friend, you are now very gloomy and sad, but if you will become a child again, even as I am, you will have a bright circlet such as I have.' When I heard that, I was so angry with myself and with the child, that I was scorched by my inward fire. Now would I fain fly up to the sun to fetch rays from him, but the rays drove me back with these words: 'Return thither whence thou camest, thou dark fire of envy, for the sun lightens only in love; the greedy earth, indeed, sometimes turns his mild light into scorching fire. Fly back, then, for with thy like alone must thou dwell.' I fell, and when I recovered myself, I was glimmering coldly above the stagnant waters."

While they were talking, the Child had fallen asleep; for he knew nothing of the world nor of men, and he could make nothing of their stories. Weariness had spoken a more intelligible language to him — *that* he understood, and had fallen asleep.

XII.

SOFTLY AND SOUNDLY he slept till the rosy morning clouds stood upon the mountain, and announced the coming of their lord, the sun. But as soon as the tidings spread over field and wood, the thousand-voiced echo awoke, and sleep was no more to be thought of.

And soon did the royal sun himself arise; at first, his dazzling diadem alone appeared above the mountains; at length, he stood upon their summit in the full majesty of his beauty, in all the charms of eternal youth, bright and glorious, his kindly glance embracing every creature of earth, from the stately oak to the blade of grass bending under the foot of the wayfaring man.

Then arose from every breast, from every throat, the joyous song of praise; and it was as if the whole plain and wood were become a temple, whose roof was the heaven, whose altar the mountain, whose congregation all creatures, whose priest the sun.

But the Child walked forth and was glad, for the birds sang sweetly, and it seemed to him as if every thing sported and danced out of mere joy to be alive. Here flew two finches through the thicket, and, twittering, pursued each other; there, the young buds burst asunder, and the tender leaves peeped out and expanded themselves in the warm sun, as if they would abide in his glance for ever; here, a dew-drop trembled, sparkling and twinkling on a blade of grass, and knew not that beneath him stood a little moss who was thirsting after him; there, troops of flies flew aloft, as if they would soar far, far over the wood: and so all was life and motion, and the Child's heart joyed to see it.

He sat down on a little smooth plot of turf, shaded by the branches of a nut-bush, and thought he should now sip the cup of his delight, drop by drop. And first he plucked down some brambles which threatened him with their prickles; then he bent aside some branches which concealed the view; then he removed the stones, so that he might stretch out his feet at full length on the soft turf; and when he had done all this, he bethought himself what was yet to do; and as he found nothing, he stood up to look for his acquaintance the dragonfly, and to beg her to guide him once more out of the wood into the open fields. About midway he met her, and she began to excuse herself for having fallen asleep in the night. The Child thought not of the past, were it even but a minute ago, so earnestly did he now wish to get out from among the thick and close trees; for his heart beat high, and he felt as if he should breathe freer in the open ground. The dragonfly flew on before and shewed him the way as far as the outermost verge of the wood, whence the Child could espy his own little hut, and then flew away to her playfellows.

XIII.

THE CHILD WALKED forth alone upon the fresh, dewy corn-field. A thousand little suns glittered in his eyes, and a lark soared warbling above his head. And the lark proclaimed the joys of the coming year, and awakened endless hopes, while she soared circling higher and higher, till, at length, her song was like the soft whisper of an angel holding converse with the spring, under the blue arch of heaven. The Child had seen the earth-coloured little bird rise up before him, and it seemed to him as if the earth had sent her forth from her bosom as a messenger to carry her joy and her thanks up to the sun, because he had turned his beaming countenance again upon her in love and bounty. And the lark hung poised above the hope-giving field, and warbled her clear and joyous song.

She sang of the loveliness of the rosy dawn, and the fresh brilliancy of the earliest sunbeams; of the gladsome springing of the young flowers, and the vigorous shooting of the corn; and her song pleased the Child beyond measure.

But the lark wheeled in higher and higher circles, and her song sounded softer and sweeter.

And now she sang of the first delights of early love; of wanderings together on the sunny, fresh hill-tops, and of the sweet pictures and visions that arise out of the blue and misty distance. The Child understood not rightly what he heard, and fain would he have understood, for he thought that even in such visions must be wondrous delight. He gazed aloft after the unwearied bird, but she had disappeared in the morning mist.

Then the Child leaned his head on one shoulder to listen if he could no longer hear the little messenger of spring; and he could just catch the distant and quivering notes in which she sang of the fervent longing after the clear element of freedom; after the pure, all-present light; and of the blessed foretaste of this desired enfranchisement, of this blending in the sea of celestial happiness.

Yet longer did he listen; for the tones of her song carried him there, where, as yet, his thoughts had never reached, and he felt himself happier in this short and imperfect flight than ever he had felt before. But the lark now dropped suddenly to the earth, for her little body was too heavy for the ambient æther, and her wings were not large nor strong enough for the pure element.

Then the red corn-poppies laughed at the homely looking bird, and cried to one another and to the surrounding blades of corn, in a shrill voice, "Now, indeed, you may see what comes of flying so high, and striving and straining after mere air; people only lose their time, and bring back nothing but weary wings and an empty stomach. That vulgar-looking ill-dressed little creature would fain raise herself above us all, and has kept up a mighty noise. And now there she lies on the ground and can hardly breathe, while we have stood still where we are sure of a good meal, and have staid like people of sense where there is something substantial to be had; and in the time she has been fluttering and singing, we have grown a good deal taller and fatter."

The other little red-caps chattered and screamed their assent so loud, that the Child's ears tingled, and he wished he could chastise them for their spiteful jeers; when a cyane said, in a soft voice, to her younger playmates, "Dear friends, be not led astray by outward show, nor by discourse, which regards only outward show. The lark is, indeed, weary, and the space into which she has soared is void; but the void is not what the lark sought, nor is the seeker returned empty home. She strove after light and freedom, and light and freedom has she proclaimed. She left the earth and its enjoyments, but she has drunk of the pure air of heaven, and has seen that it is not the earth, but the sun that is steadfast. And if earth has called her back, it can keep nothing of her but what is its own. Her sweet voice and her soaring wings belong to the sun, and will enter into light and freedom, long after the foolish prater shall have sunk and been buried in the dark prison of the earth."

And the lark heard her wise and friendly discourse, and with renewed strength, she sprang once more into the clear and beautiful blue.

Then the Child clapped his little hands for joy, that the sweet bird had flown up again, and that the red-caps must hold their tongues for shame.

XIV.

And the Child was become happy and joyful, and breathed freely again, and thought no more of returning to his hut, for he saw that nothing returned inwards, but rather that all strove outwards into the free air; the rosy apple blossoms from their narrow buds, and the gurgling notes from the narrow breast of the lark. The germs burst open the folding doors of the seeds, and broke through the heavy pressure of the earth in order to get at the light: the grasses tore asunder their bands, and their slender blades sprung upwards. Even the rocks were become gentle, and allowed little mosses to peep out from their sides, as a sign that they would not remain impenetrably closed for ever. And the flowers sent out colour and fragrance into the whole world, for they kept not their best for themselves, but would imitate the sun and the stars, which poured their warmth and radiance over the spring. And many a little gnat and beetle burst the narrow cell in which it was enclosed, and crept out slowly, and, half asleep, unfolded and shook its tender wings, and soon gained strength, and flew off to untried delights.

And as the butterflies came forth from their chrysalids in all their gaiety and splendour, so did every humbled and suppressed aspiration and hope free itself, and boldly launch into the open and flowing sea of spring.

Commentary on Carové's Kinderleben oder das Mährchen ohne Ende

FRIEDRICH WILHELM CAROVÉ (1789-1852) has remained little known in spite of a considerable number of publications, mostly of the philosophical-essayistic type.[1] He was born a Catholic in Koblenz where he studied law; after that he held various positions as a customs official in the Rhine area. These positions enabled him to devote time to a variety of cultural studies. He contributed, for instance, to the philological endeavors of Jacob and Wilhelm Grimm and corresponded with them, with Ludwig Tieck, and with many other Romantics. Carové's many poems, stories, essays, and reviews appeared in a variety of journals. From 1816 to 1818 he studied with Hegel in Heidelberg and obtained the doctorate. There he helped Victor Cousin understand Hegel's *Enzyklopädie der philosophischen Wissenschaften* (*Encyclopedia of the Philosophical Sciences*). Sarah Austin, the English translator of the story by Carové published in this volume, met Cousin in Bonn in 1827 and came to admire his writings greatly. Her translation of Cousin's *De l'instruction publique dans quelques pays de l'Allemagne, et particulièrement en Prusse* as *Report on the State of Public Instruction in Prussia* appeared in 1834, the same year as her translation of Carové's story. It is not unlikely that Cousin called Austin's attention to Carové. Carové was a leader of the Heidelberg *Burschenschaft*, the liberal student organization at the time, and made an important speech at the historic meeting on the Wartburg in 1817. He also explained the murder of the antiliberal playwright August von Kotzebue by a student along Hegelian lines, thus running afoul of the Prussian authorities who saw to it that he would not receive an appointment as a professor. Carové had a number of positions for a few years but soon devoted himself exclusively to philosophical, historical, religious, and literary studies, in all of which he tried to translate, in the spirit of Hegel, the Catholic faith of his youth into a pan-European humanism.

---

[1] The most recent study is by me, "Friedrich Wilhelm Carové, Autor eines einzigartigen Kunstmärchens," in: *Autoren damals und heute. Literaturgeschichtliche Beispiele veränderter Wirkungshorizonte*, ed. Gerhard P. Knapp. Amsterdam, Atlanta, Ga.: Rodopi, 1991, pp. 133-53 (Amsterdamer Beiträge zur neueren Germanistik, volume 31-33).

Carové was familiar with the medieval and late medieval literature of Germany, France, Italy, and Spain and translated and adapted poems and stories from these sources. His first collection, *Romantische Blätter* (Eisenach, 1818; Romantic Leaves), contained a number of stories that combined a pseudo-medieval world with a rather shallow Christian morality. Carové published an earlier version of the final sections of *Kinderleben oder das Mährchen ohne Ende* on the last twelve pages of *Romantische Blätter*. I will return to this fragment below.

The Christian element is even more pronounced in Carové's second collection, entitled *Moosblüthen* (Frankfurt am Main, 1830; Moss Blossoms). There are three "Christabends=Erzählungen" (Christmas Eve Stories), a love story that takes place on the tower of the city of Andernach (where Carové had been a customs official), and thirty-three poems whose main theme is love, pure Christian love; most of the poems are sonnets and none is distinguished. Carové uses forms ("Peine" instead of *Pein*) and word order ("Jungfrau reine" instead of *reine Jungfrau*) that made his diction sound artificial, an aspect that a reviewer already at the time found objectionable.[2] Carové undoubtedly had the symbolic associations of the number fourteen (the double of seven), the number of lines of his sonnets, in mind when he divided *Kinderleben oder das Mährchen ohne Ende* into fourteen sections.

Interspersed in *Moosblüthen* are six plates that Carové, according to the preface, had a "jungen hoffnungsvollen Künstler, Herrn Becker von Darmstadt" cut for the volume.[3] The frontispiece is a Christ child by Johannes Valdor (Jean Waldor), the other five are vignettes by Philipp Otto Runge that the artist made for Ludwig Tieck's *Minnelieder aus dem Schwäbischen Zeitalter* (1803; Love Songs from the Swabian, i.e., Medieval Period). Tieck had translated the medieval po-

---

[2] *Jenaer Allgemeine Literatur-Zeitung*, no. 42 (March 1832), 335-36.

[3] J.B.C. Grundy ("Runge and Carové. An Unpublished Document of the Romantik," *Art Bulletin*, 16 [1934], 25-26) identifies the initial of the engraver as an "F" and Jörg Traeger (*Philipp Otto Runge und sein Werk. Monographie und kritischer Katalog*. Munich: Prestel, 1975, p. 341) follows him. However, the initial could also be a "J" which would make it possible to credit a Jakob Becker with the engravings. According to Thieme-Becker, a Jakob Becker was born in 1810 and worked as a lithographer in Frankfurt am Main at the time when *Moosblüthen* was published (1830). Thus, Carové's characterization of Becker as *hoffnungsvoll* (promising) would fit. However, Carové's "aus Darmstadt" would not since Jakob Becker was born in Dittelsheim (near Worms). I have not found any other Becker who could be considered.

ems into modern German. He was an admirer of Runge and was impressed by his combination of children and flowers and the meaning of these designs. While Becker's reproductions of Runge's designs have been called clumsy and inaccurate, Carové has been praised by art historians for having selected vignettes by Runge at a time when his fame had already very much faded.[4] In his preface Carové refers to the "reichen Garten des unsterblichen *Runge*" (the rich store [of art work] of the immortal Runge). While in Tieck's edition of medieval poems one can see a direct connection between vignettes and poems only in the case of the poem Tieck wrote himself, there is always a close relationship between the vignette and Carové's poem or story that followed the vignette.

In the center of Runge's vignettes are children, always in connection with flowers. One of the vignettes immediately precedes *Kinderleben oder das Mährchen ohne Ende*. Runge himself described that particular vignette as follows:

> ein Kind hält sich selbst eine kleine Rose vor, aus welcher ein Engelchen hervorkommt, es sitzt dabey unter dem Schirmdach einer Lilie, die mit ihren Stabfäden sich zu dem Namen Jehovah's in einer Engelglorie hinbeugt. (A child holds in front a small rose out of which a little angel emerges; the child sits under the protective roof of a lily that bends with its stamens toward the name of Jehovah surrounded by angelic glory.)[5]

The Runge vignette seems to have served Carové as a point of departure for his story. In both the vignette and the story a child of undetermined sex forms the center. There is in both an intimate relationship between the child and flowers. In section four of the story the child is greeted by a rose which loves to be mirrored in the blooming head of a child with whom it likes to share its heart's secrets. In the same section, as on the vignette, a lily bends toward the child. The lily is looking up to the sun and the sun looks into the lily's calyx, and the golden stamens unite in the center. In this moment the child in Carové's story overhears a little divine animal at the bottom of the lily's calyx say "now will the mystery be fulfilled [...] as [...] the dim image of his unknown parents, as it were veiled in a holy light, floated before his eyes."[6] We have here clearly a mystical moment in

---

[4] J. B. C. Grundy, see note 3, p. 23.

[5] Philipp Otto Runge, *Hinterlassene Schriften*, ed. by his older brother. First Part. Hamburg: Perthes, 1840, p. 236, rpt. Göttingen: Vandenhoeck & Ruprecht, 1965 (Deutsche Neudrucke: Reihe Texte des 19. Jahrhunderts).

[6] Here, as elsewhere, I am using Sarah Austin's translation.

the child's life. In the description of his vignettes from which I quoted above, Runge specifically refers to Jakob Böhme, the seventeenth-century mystic, whose writings played an important role among the Romantics.

The child in Carové's story lives alone, without any contact whatever with other people. The only reference to other people we find out is to the unknown parents in the passage I just quoted. Later on we read that behind the hut lie flower beds that are unattended but that plenty of flowers still thrive there. These beds are surrounded by palm branches that were placed there many years ago. From the *Handwörterbuch des Aberglaubens* (E. Hoffmann-Krayer, ed. Berlin and Leipzig: de Gruyter, 1927-1942, vol. VI, pp. 1374-76) we learn that palm branches are used to insure a good crop and to keep the hail away. We also read in the story that the child has a sheep. The child is ignorant about people and the world; flowers and animals and even a drop of water will teach the child about life in the course of the story.

Carové begins his story in the fairy tale style with "Es war einmal" and continues with a phrase in which the initial *das* is a demonstrative and therefore does not push the verb to the end. Both the opening phrase and the special construction following it were made popular by the brothers Grimm. The child is awakened by the rays of the sun and the song of the birds and, without looking at the mirror, which, with the hut, the bed, and the remains of a flower garden are the only man-made objects mentioned in the story, ventures out and eats breakfast gathered from various flowers. The child, while walking through a meadow and then through the woods, will come across some thirty-two different flowers and plants and eighteen different animals. Plants, animals, and inanimate objects and the child can talk to each other, with the plants, animals, and the inanimate objects taking on human characteristics. One soon sees through Carové's value system. The bee is criticized for storing its wealth without enjoying it, while the butterfly, having left behind its earthbound stage, is praised: it playfully takes delight in the air and light and listens to the conversations of the flowers. Also criticized is the wave for thinking it could be like the stars as are the mouse and the lizard for having evil tongues. There are the malicious mosquitoes, some of which keep the child from falling asleep in the cave and are then killed by a spider, and there are the will-o'-the-wisps that only think of themselves. They did not heed a Christ-like figure and were therefore condemned to hover above swamps as *Irrlichter*, i.e., lights that literally have gone astray. And finally, in the last section, the lark is praised for its striving upward, toward the sun, toward light, even if its endeavors are in vain, while the earthbound, materialistic corn poppies are put down. They are the only flowers that are criticized.

The dragonfly — the German word *Libelle* has a much lovelier association — takes over as the child's guide. I have already referred to the mystical moment when the lily and the sun exchange glances. When the child is looking at the leaves and the sky and their reflection in a pond and wonders which one of the two are the true leaves and the true sky and whether the below was there for the benefit of the above or vice versa, the dragonfly explains that leaves and sky and their reflections exist for each other only in the eyes of the child and that they are true only in the child's thoughts since these thoughts could appropriate them.

The dragonfly also sees to it that the child sleeps safely in a cave. Harmony between the child and nature is expressed clearly in the ancient symbol of the cave which carries the association with the protective womb. In addition, there are the fireflies (*Johannisfünklein*) that hear about the great flower with two lovely stars, i.e., the child with its eyes, and that believe that that flower must be their king. They fly to the cave and illuminate it so brightly that the child is delighted. In Johann Jacob Christoph von Grimmelshausen's *Continuatio* to the *Simplicissimus* (1669) fireflies — here of unusually large size — play a similar role and are also used symbolically with a Christian meaning. There is a legend found in Southern Italy according to which the Lord sent a firefly to light up the cave of a prisoner (*Handwörterbuch des Aberglaubens*, vol. IV, p. 764). One could place Carové's story, then, on June 24th, the day of John the Baptist with whom the *Johannisfünklein* are associated. June 24 would also fit the season in which the story takes place, i.e., spring which is the last word with which both the German and English versions end.

In the morning the child witnesses a thoroughly Romantic moment in which nature forms the church, altar, priest, and congregation, and the sun is the holiest or the eye of God. When the blue cornflower praises the lark's striving for light and freedom since the sun and not the earth is what is permanent, the child is delighted and decides not to go back to the dark and confining hut. Now is the time for a general awakening and nature's breaking out into the freedom of a new beginning with its splendid display of colors, smells, and sounds. The story ends with a paean to nature and its renewal in spring and thus can truly be called one "without an end."

I already mentioned the fairy tale type construction with which Carové begins the story. The many diminutives also belong to a style that imitates fairy tale and folksong. The spelling of "Mährchen" with an "h" was widespread at the beginning of the century and can be found in the writings of the Grimm brothers and Ludwig Tieck, among others. There are many constructions that attempt to present the world in a child-like manner. In section three one finds "Kämmerlein," "streckte sein Händchen nach dem nächsten Sternlein aus," "war der Mond seines Weges gewandert [...] hinter den Berg schlafen gegangen" and in section ten "als es mit dem Schlafen gar nicht gehen wollte, richtete es sich auf, um zu warten, bis es dem Herrn Schlaf gefällig wäre zu kommen." Carové uses the quaint "klungen" (section 8) to give the story an old-fashioned tone. Then there are the many poetic expressions and devices, such as alliteration ("sein Mahl mundete ihm" [section 1], "dufteten um die Wette, und jeder Wohlklang nahm einen Wohlgeruch bei der Hand" [section 5]), use of proverbs and idioms ("Da fühlte ich wohl, der Hochmuth komme vor dem Fall," "so ward mir hier nun auch das Salz der Demuth zu Theil" [section 2]) as well as similes ("waren die Töne der Nachtigall fliegende Maiblumen, oder die Maiblumen sichtbare, als Tropfen herabgethaute, Nachtigalltöne" [section 5]). In the last example there is also synaesthesia. Carové's consciously poetic language is equally noticeable in the rhymed pairs "wellte und quellte" (section 2) and "wegsam und regsam" (section 8).

I have mentioned above a fragmentary, earlier version of *Kinderleben oder das Mährchen ohne Ende*. The earlier version is found in *Romantische Blätter* (1818, pp. 251-64) and is entitled "Aus einem fortgehenden Mährchen." I take "fortgehend" to mean in progress. The origin of Carové's story, published in 1834, goes back, then, at least to 1818. In the fragmentary version there are two sections, the first one entitled "Die Irrlichter" (the will-o'-the-wisps), the second one "Die Lerche" (the lark). The first corresponds to the end of section ten and almost all of section eleven of the 1834 text, that is, basically the stories of the two will-o'-the-wisps. The second contains almost all of section thirteen, i.e., the lark's celebration of spring and universal love. Carové made a number of stylistic changes, replacing a temporal "wie" by an "als" and taking out but also adding a few words such as the description of the "Cyane" as "eben frisch aufgeblühte, himmelblaue Cyane" (the sky-blue cornflower that just had come into bloom). There are no substantive changes; however, the many small ones attest to the care Carové spent on the story.

The child-like, fairy tale style of the story contrasts with the learned "Cyane" (section 13) and with such passages as the one I already mentioned when the child wonders about which of the images is the true one, the sky and the leaves above the pond or their reflections in it and the sophisticated explanation given by the dragonfly. Similarly, we have "Das *Singende* aber und das *Auffliegende* in ihr [the lark] gehört schon der Sonne an, und wird dort eingehen in das Licht und die Freiheit" (section 13). Also transgressing the child-like world and language is the ending of the story to which I referred above, the blue cornflower's praise of song and upward flight as well as the paean to spring.

Kinderleben oder das Mährchen ohne Ende belongs, then, to the genre of *Kunstmärchen*, a tale by an author who incorporates in its language and contents a number of fairy tale characteristics but also specific philosophical ideas. Carové's story comes at the end of the Romantic period and has antecedents in such works as Novalis's fairy tale "Hyacinth und Rosenblüte" which forms part of *Die Lehrlinge zu Sais* (1802; *The Novices of Sais*) where Hyacinth, the young man, spends all his time in nature and can understand flowers and animals. Cyane, the blue cornflower of section thirteen of Carové's story, has its antecedent in the name of the beloved in the second, fragmentary part of Novalis's *Heinrich von Ofterdingen* (1802). Carové expressed his high esteem of Novalis as late as 1838 in his *Neorama* (Leipzig: Wigand, p. 105). The fragmentary part of *Heinrich von Ofterdingen* was published by Ludwig Tieck whose *Die Elfen* (1811; *The Elves*) also shows similarities to Carové's story. Most closely related is E. T. A. Hoffmann's *Das fremde Kind* (1817; *The Strange Child*), specifically the passage when the "fremde Kind" — the child from afar — visits Felix and Christlieb and all three understand the flowers, the trees, and the brook. They then start flying like birds and see the child's beautiful castles in the air. In Hoffmann's story, though, there is the constant tension to the world of everyday reality to which Felix and Christlieb have to return. A narrator tells Hoffmann's story which then receives comments by the listeners. One of them remarks that *Das fremde Kind* could be called a fairy tale for little and big children while another listener suggests that it is a fairy tale for children and for those who are not children. The same could be said of Carové's story. Of course, his story in no way reaches the intellectual intricacies and aesthetic perfection of either Novalis, Tieck or Hoffmann. Published after *Kinderleben oder das Mährchen ohne Ende* and showing striking similarities to it is Hans Christian Andersen's *Thumbeling* (*Little Thumb*). In Andersen's tale a tiny girl, who for most of the tale is not connected to any other human being, lives among animals and flowers that have, as in Carové's story, positive and negative characteristics. The girl finally marries a prince who is surrounded by flowers.

Kinderleben oder das Mährchen ohne Ende shows a prelapsarian world in which there is relative harmony between the child and all of nature; there are also pronounced religious and philosophical aspects to the story. I have already pointed out the Christ-like figures who appear to the will-o'-the-wisps and try to correct their sinful ways. I have also mentioned above the scene in which we find the child, who in the morning has left the cave, in a church-like natural surrounding with the sun being God's eye. One could furthermore say that the general tone is one of ethical Christianity in that helping, giving, and sharing are praised over selfishness, overbearing pride, and hoarding. As a student of idealistic philosophy Carové emphasizes becoming when he has, for instance, the butterfly transform its earlier earthbound existence into one of a "higher" kind where freedom reigns. Also reflecting idealism is the assertion of the centrality of the mind when the child is told by the dragonfly that the child's thought is permanent, not the material world. Many other passages reveal a similar world-view.

Kinderleben oder das Mährchen ohne Ende is, then, a very special example of a late Romantic *Kunstmärchen* as defined by Jens Tismar: a story by an author who in telling the story incorporates both fairy tale aspects and the author's specific poetic ideas. The story also shows the restitution of a world of harmony among all of nature, including people, and is written in a language that is consciously literary. However, Tismar finds that the typical Romantic *Kunstmärchen* shows a world in which the alienation between humans and nature is only partially or temporarily undone.[7] In Carové's story, on the other hand, there is, except for the child's vague longing for his or her unknown parents, never any question about the fact that the harmonious world in which the child lives is the only world and that it will remain forever part of that world. In that respect and in presenting the unnamed child without any human contact Carové's story is indeed unique.

---

[7] Jens Tismar, *Kunstmärchen* (Stuttgart: Metzler, 1977), p. 31.

Commentary on Austin's The Story Without an End

CAROVÉ WAS MOST fortunate in having Sarah Austin as the translator of his story.[8] He could not have asked for a more qualified person. By 1834 she had established herself as one of the most accomplished and respected translators of works written in German and French. In a letter dated 23 May 1834 Carové expresses surprise at receiving the book and delight with her translation. According to him, the two versions "if placed side by side, they might be hailed as twins." He also mentions the "charming dedication" and the importance of early childhood impressions.[9]

Sarah Taylor was born in Norwich in 1793, received an excellent education, learned German at an early age, and in 1819 married John Austin who was to become a noted legal scholar. Their only child Lucie was born in 1821. In 1827 the Austins went to Bonn so that John

---

[8] The basic study is by Lotte and Joseph Hamburger, *Troubled Lives. John and Sarah Austin* (Toronto, Buffalo, London: University of Toronto Press, 1985). Her "affair by correspondence" with Fürst Pückler-Muskau is described in detail by the same authors in *Contemplating Adultery. The Secret Life of a Victorian Woman* (New York: Fawcett Columbine, 1991). For Sarah Austin and Germany see Heinrich Mutschmann, "Sarah Austin und die deutsche Literatur," *Die Neueren Sprachen*, 27 (1919), 97-128 and D. F. S. Scott, "Sarah Austin and Germany," *GLL*, n.s., 2 (1949), 138-48. About to appear at the Edwin Melln Press is my "Sarah Austin's Assessment of Goethe's Character and Works and of Weimar," in a volume edited by Gerhart Hoffmeister entitled *Weimar Classicism: Reassessment and Reception*.

[9] The original letter has been lost as have been many letters to Austin from a number of German intellectuals. See Werner Vordtriede, "Bettina's englisches Wagnis," *Euphorion*, 51 (1957), 276. One sentence of Carové's letter is quoted by Sigmund Münz in "Briefe Ottilie Goethe's und Anderer an Sarah Austin," *Neue freie Presse*, Vienna, 12 January 1895, Feuilleton. Carové uses here the same flowery, *kitschig* language he used in the preface to *Moosblüthen*: "Ich erröthete fast wie ein Maiblümchen die Augen niederschlagen würde, wenn es sich in eine reich vergoldete Blumenvase versetzt fände." The English translation of Carové's letter is found in Janet Ross, *Three Generations of Englishwomen. Memoirs and Correspondence of Mrs. John Taylor, Mrs. Sarah Austin, and Lady Duff Gordon*, 2 vols. (London: Murray, 1888), I, pp. 86-87.

could prepare his lectures at the University of London. Upon their return to London the following year it became clear that he could not attract a sufficient number of students. Therefore, he had to resign his chair. John rarely had an income adequate to the family's needs. He was, in contrast to Sarah, extremely withdrawn and ill at ease with people. Sarah saw in writing, especially in translating, a way to supplement their income. While in Germany, she made many acquaintances among German intellectuals. Thomas Carlyle, in a letter to his wife, dated 30 August 1831, describes Sarah in the following way:

> Mrs. A (her Husband is Professor of Law in the despised and despicable London University) is the most enthusiastic of German Mystics I have met with: an exceedingly vivid person, not without insight, but enthusiastic, as it were astonished rapt to ecstacy with the German Apocalypse; she says herself *verdeutscht*.

Austin achieved a great success with her translation of Fürst Pückler-Muskau's account of his travels in Great Britain (*Briefe eines Verstorbenen*) as *Tour in England, Ireland, and France in the Years 1828 and 1829 [...] by a German Prince* (London, 1832). Subsequently, she translated many other works from the German, notably two long works by Leopold von Ranke (1840, 1845), a series of biographical sketches of Goethe, Duke Karl August and Duchess Luise (1833), and *Fragments from German Prose Writers* (1841). John Herman Merivale in a review of her *Characteristics of Goethe*, while finding fault with her choice of sources, has nothing but "admiration of the truly extraordinary manner in which she has rendered all their various contents" and that in the case of the *Tour in England* "many people persisted in believing the work to have been manufactured at home, merely because the language did not offer the slightest traces of transfusion from a foreign original."[10] Austin died in 1867.

The only complete literary work, except for a few poems, Austin translated was Carové's *Kinderleben oder das Mährchen ohne Ende* as *The Story Without an End*. According to the dedication she read the story first in German to her daughter Lucie who was fluent in that language and who, as Lady Duff Gordon, was to become, as her mother, a noted translator and author. She counted Carové's story among her favorites during all of her life. According to Austin, her daughter wanted English children who did not understand German to enjoy the story, too. Both Janet Ross, Lucie's daughter, and Katherine Frank in her most readable biography of Lady Duff Gordon, mention Lucie's

---

[10] John Herman Merivale, "Sarah Austin's *Characteristics of Goethe*," *Edinburgh Review*, 57 (1833), 372.

love of animals and how, as a child, she longed to be able to converse with flowers. Carové's story is written, of course, to satisfy such longings in the fictional world of a fairy tale.[11] Carové in his preface had referred readers to Runge's vignettes as a compensation for the poor quality of the contents of *Moosblüthen*. Maybe by coincidence and maybe not, Austin in the dedication to Lucie hopes "that, if others think the story less beautiful than you do, they may find compensation in the graceful designs it has inspired." She refers here to the illustrations by William Harvey that I will discuss below.

I already mentioned Carové's grateful reaction when he acknowledged receipt of her translation of his story. Carlyle wrote on 21 January 1834 upon receiving a copy of the book: "It is an *allerliebstes Büchlein* [a most delightful little book], graceful in spirit as in embodyment [sic] and decoration; and we all participate in Lucy's [Lucie's] love of it."

As several of Austin's letter from 1829 and 1830 to John Murray, the publisher, make clear, she was eager to have him publish children's literature, be that in book form or as a periodical. She would translate the material from the German. In an undated letter to him she also suggested that he publish what from internal evidence must be identified as her translation of Carové's *Kinderleben oder das Mährchen ohne Ende*. Since the letter shows Austin's excellent understanding of the German original and how it differed from the more "matter of factness" of the children's literature favored in England at the time and since the letter is unpublished, here is the full text:

> Dear Sir, The MS. you have sent me, & which you receive herewith, has suggested to me the thought of troubling you with one of mine. This is hardly fair upon you but I hope you will forgive the inappropriateness of the time I have chosen as my story is for much older children than your author's *Little Charles*. I translated this from the German some time ago & have suffered it to lie in my portfolio from hopelessness of finding a *children's publisher* who would at all understand a thing so unlike the routine children's books of England, the characteristics of which is *matter of factness*. They are admirable in their way, & teach a vast number of things but it seems to me there is something wanting for the cultivation of high sentiments & enlarged affections — the German children's books teach much less, but they are addressed most beneficially to the heart & imagination. If you will do me the favour to look over this enchanting (as

---

[11] Janet Ross, *Three Generations of Englishwomen* (see above, note 9), vol. II, pp. 174-75, and Katherine Frank, *A Passage to Egypt. The Life of Lady Duff Gordon* (Boston, New York: Houghton, Mifflin, 1994), p. 32.

I feel it) & strange composition you will see what I mean. All the appearances of Nature are described not scientifically or practically, as with us, but with an enthusiastic love for the beautiful and the elevated which is really affecting. Above all, every creature is regarded with reference to the Source & kind of its creation, & all this is done with such poetry & luxuriant feeling that it has the charm & interest of a fairy tale. It has been handed about among my friends till it is so dirty I am ashamed to send it. I have copied Chapter I which was full of *corrections*. If you *do* look at it, let me entreat the favour of you to read the last two or three chapters without which no adequate idea can be formed of it. I had thought of sending it to an annual but I am told that they are so temporary that I relinquished the idea. If you thought it fit to publish it, I would find two or three other stories & make a little Volume.[12]

I have not been able to identify *Little Charles*. The letter by Austin is in the John Murray Archive in London and has an added "1830?" at the top. If that is correct, it took Austin another four years to have the story published, not by John Murray but by Effingham Wilson. Austin's comments on the story make clear that she sees in the last sections with their criticism of materialism and the praise of idealistic thriving and of nature's eternal renewal the essential aspects of *The Story Without an End*.

By selecting *Kinderleben oder das Mährchen ohne Ende* from among the various stories contained in *Moosblüthen* Austin showed excellent judgment: the story is by far the most unusual and the least didactic of those in the collection and the only one that could have had an appeal to the English reader. Her English version reads very well justifying the praise contemporaries bestowed on her work as a translator. By omitting the first part of the title she arouses the curiosity of the reader. Her rendering is, as it should be for the purpose, a free one, imitating the style of the original but not in a slavish way. Occasionally she uses, as Carové had done, an older form such as "knowest thou" (section 4) and "spake" (section 7). The sex-neutral *Kind* of the original is a boy in Austin's version even though she dedicated the story to her daughter. Still, as the section on the illustrations will show, four of the eight illustrators of *The Story Without an End* opted for a sex-neutral child. At times Austin adds an alliteration to compensate for those instances when there was one in the German text but she was unable to find an English equivalent ("striving and straining" for "Streben" [section 13]). In a few cases Austin simplifies

---

[12] I want to thank John Murray, London, for the authorization to publish the letter.

the text as when she renders "mit einem kaiserlichen Kometen=Prinzen Hochzeit halten" as "nuptials [...] with the prince of the sun" (section 8). In section 4 the currant's pleading to be eaten first by the child and in section 11 details of the fate of the second will-o'-the-wisp are omitted, also, one assumes, for the sake of simplification. Strangely enough, Austin keeps the word "Cyane" of the original, a word that is changed in later editions to cornflower (section 13). When the child eats red currants and in the original Saint John is mentioned in connection with them, she explains in a note that that berry is called in German *Johannisbeere* (section 4).

Austin misunderstands some of the German phrases: "kam ich mit [...] einem blauen Auge davon" becomes "I escaped with [...] a black eye" (section 2, it should be: I got off cheaply, with a small loss), "fast wären die Augen ihm übergegangen" becomes "as if his eyes were weary with trying to look through it" (section 7, for the correct translation see below), and for "Wie nun das Sandmännchen dem Kinde kleine Aeuglein machte" Austin has "But as the child saw the ant peeping up at him" (section 10, it should be: As the child was getting sleepy). Even J. C. Pickard in his generally more accurate, but also more prosaic version of Carové's story (Chicago: Winchell, 1885) translated only the second of the three passages Austin misunderstood correctly: "tears had almost come into his eyes." The above are the few major mistakes Austin made, most everything else she translated accurately and beautifully.

The list of editions at the end of this volume will give evidence of the success Austin's version had in the English-speaking world. Of these thirteen appeared in England, and eighteen in the United States. All but twelve appeared between 1889 and 1913. Heath had first published the story in 1902, then again in 1909. It was to keep it in print until 1935. Thus, new editions did not appear after 1913 when World War I turned the English-reading public against idealistic fantasy literature of German origin.

The success of *The Story Without an End* can be measured not only by the many editions but also by the fact that in 1842 appeared by a certain C. M. *The Child and the Hermit; or a Sequel to the Story Without an End* (London: Darton & Clark). The anonymous author claims that a friend said that "'The Story without an End' [...] — notwithstanding the attractive style, and the sweet descriptions of Nature's favourites with which it abounds, — that some parts are veiled in much obscurity, and that 'The Story' is more suited to the imaginative character of the Germans, than to the mind of an English child" (pp. vii-viii). The author then points to the fact that Carové's title is open-ended, and that therefore a continuation is suggested. There is also a summary of the contents of *The Story Without an End* for those who are not familiar with it. Two years later, in 1844, Anna Moline translated another of Carové's stories from *Moosblüthen*, *The Story of Gottfried and Beata* and identified Carové on the tile page as the "Author of the Story without an End" (London: Harvey and Darton). Neither *The Child and the Hermit* nor *The Story of Gottfried and Beata* was successful. There were also German language editions of Carové's story as *Das Mährchen ohne Ende* for the use of teaching the language that included notes and vocabulary (London: Senior, 1841; London, Leipzig: Thimm, 1852; New York: Holt, 1864). As is typical for such editions, the text was changed in a few places.

The type of text, also its brevity, made it attractive to the private presses. Thomas Bird Mosher, the well-known printer of Portland, Maine, published Carové's story first in 1897 and then three more times. There is also a beautiful edition, with a dedication to his daughter by John Harnby, printed at the Ashendene Press. Occasionally *The Story Without an End* was published together with other stories, as *The Glow-worm* (a second-rate Sunday school tale, see Bibliography, no. 3), a number of English and German stories, selected undoubtedly for being suitable for children (see Bibliography, no. 4), and with Adelbert von Chamisso's *Peter Schlemihl* and Novalis's *Hymnen an die Nacht* (see Bibliography, no. 6). Most of the editions keep Austin's dedication to her daughter and several of those I inspected were bound with elaborately designed covers.

The *Story Without an End*, then, had many appreciative readers and listeners "of six feet high, and lower stature," as Carlyle predicted it would have in his letter to Austin of 21 January 1834. Thus, a remarkable work of late Romanticism was absorbed by thousands of English-speaking children. In his informative study of the *Kunstmärchen*, Friedmar Apel tells of the success of the English translation of the *Kinder- und Hausmärchen* beginning with the publication of the first part in 1823. Apel claims, though, that the Grimm fairy tales were read by and large in the moral and didactic tradition of the English attitude toward children that saw in them small adults. Apel further says that the English versions of the *Kunstmärchen* Thomas Carlyle translated were not received with empathy: "Eine fruchtbare Rezeption der romantischen Konzeption des Phantastischen in der Form des Kunstmärchens hat es auf direkt nachweisbarem Wege auch später nie gegeben" (A fruitful reception [in England] of the romantic conception of the fantastic in the form of the *Kunstmärchen* cannot be proven, not even at a later time).[13] From the preceding it will have become clear that Austin's *The Story Without an End* needs to be mentioned here as an important link between the German *Kunstmärchen* and the English-reading public.

---

[13] Friedmar Apel, *Die Zaubergärten der Phantasie. Zur Theorie und Geschichte des Kunstmärchens* (Heidelberg: Winter, 1978), p. 222.

The Prefaces

I HAVE ALREADY referred to Carové's preface to *Moosblüthen*, of which *Kinderleben oder das Mährchen ohne Ende* forms a part, and to Austin's dedication of her translation to her daughter. In a number of English editions we find prefaces. The most important of these is the one in the second edition of *The Story Without an End* that was published in Boston in 1836. The preface is by A. Bronson Alcott, the noted educator and one of the leading exponents of transcendentalism. The ideas of transcendentalism with its belief that God is immanent in man and nature agree well with those at the basis of Carové's story. Clearly, Alcott recognized a kindred soul in the author of *The Story Without an End*. Alcott saw in Carové's story the soul's introduction to the true values of life through the communion with nature and the overcoming of the senses by ascending to the spiritual. As far as I know, the connection between transcendentalism and Carové's story has never been pointed out but seems quite obvious to me.[14] It is interesting to note that Jakob Böhme, the seventeenth-century mystic, was also studied by Alcott. As I stated above, Böhme was admired by the German Romantics, among them Philipp Otto Runge who mentions Böhme in connection with the vignettes Carové selected for *Moosblüthen*. Alcott saw in *The Story Without an End* "An Emblem Of The Spiritual Life" (p. 9) and writes as follows in the preface:

---

[14] Sigrid Bauschinger in her book *Die Posaune der Reform. Deutsche Literatur im Neuengland des 19. Jahrhunderts* (Bern and Stuttgart: Francke, 1989) discusses Alcott's preface briefly and relates Carové's story to Goethe's *Das Märchen* (*The Fairy Tale*), primarily on the basis of the will-o'-the-wisps that are found in both works (p. 166). Actually, the two tales have little in common. While Bauschinger does not point out the close ideological connection between *The Story Without an End* and transcendentalism, she refers to an interesting passage in the second edition of Louisa May Alcott's novel *Moods* (1882). Here Sylvia, the protagonist, asks the beloved Adam Warwick to tell her what sort of book she was. He responds *The Story Without an End* and asks her whether she ever read it. Sylvia then says: "'Yes; I wish I might be as lovely, innocent, and true as that is. Thank you very much.'" Alcott continues: "And Sylvia put her small hand into the large one as confidingly as the child in the pretty allegory might have done." (Louisa May Alcott, *Moods*, edited and with an introduction by Sarah Elbert [New Brunswick and London: Rutgers, 1991], p. 242).

The present volume is designed to quicken the hearts of the young, by displaying to their view, in the significant Imagery of Nature, an Emblem of their Spiritual Life. Under the Type of a Child, the Soul communes with the Beautiful in the visible World, quickening whatever it beholds from its own Ideal, thus apprehending its latent faculties, their resurrection from the senses, and final ascension into the Spiritual. It is a revival, in a new form, of the beautiful fable of Psyche.

The work, it will be perceived, is a reprint of the German of Carové, as translated by Mrs. Austin. To aid the reader in apprehending the Emblem, the subject of each chapter has been given, as a key to the leading thought. For living minds this assistance, will scarce be needful.

That this, and the series of which it is the commencement, may serve to hallow the associations, and quicken the spiritual sense of the young, is the earnest desire of the Editor.

Boston, May 1836.

Subjects of the Work. [...] I. Appetite. II. Passion. III. Fancy. IV. Sentiment. V. Love. VI. Dislike. VII. Thought. VIII. Imagination. IX. Genius. X. Reason. XI. Doubt. XII. Religion. XIII. Faith. XIV. Aspiration.

(pp. iii-v)

With a bit of good will the "subjects" can be related to the contents of the chapters and the illustrations. The various "subjects" appear again under each of the fourteen illustrations by William Harvey that already formed part of the first edition. On the title page we find under the illustration by the same artist: "'Symbolical is all that meets the sense, / One mighty alphabet for infant minds.' *Coleridge.*" The quotation is an adaptation of lines 18-20 of "The Destiny of Nations. A Vision."

Thomas Bird Mosher in his foreword to the 1897 edition quotes George Saintsbury's characterization of Carové's story as being "exquisite" and claims that Sarah Austin "half adapted, half translated" it. He also refers to Walter Besant who had read *The Story Without an End* as a child and who thinks in *The Eulogy of Richard Jefferies* that Jefferies must have had Carové's work in mind when writing his own stories. Mosher then quotes from the same Carlyle letter I already referred to above. Obviously, Mosher had done his homework before publishing the story. He ends the foreword by maintaining that *The Story Without an End* with "Its old world *naiveté* still touches, even as a child's tiny fingers might touch, our human hearts."

In the 1902 edition Thomas Wentworth Higginson, the American clergyman and abolitionist, characterizes both Carové and Austin and then refers to Alcott's "quaint preface." At the end of his preface Higginson says that the story is "Reprinted for the benefit of those 'living minds' of whom Mr. Alcott speaks, and especially for young children, whose minds are always living."

Finally, in 1904, Curtis Wager-Smith directs his folksy introductory words to the child who will be enchanted by the "dear old tale that the little German children listened to, years and years and years ago."

The Illustrations

THERE IS PHILIPP Otto Runge's vignette that Carové used for *Kinderleben oder das Mährchen ohne Ende* and there are eight artists of illustrations for *The Story Without an End*. In the following I will characterize briefly the work of each one of the illustrators.

I have already mentioned Carové's selecting Philipp Otto Runge's vignettes for the volume in which *Kinderleben oder das Mährchen ohne Ende* appeared. The vignette that immediately precedes the story is reproduced in this edition. Runge's design, as I explained earlier, probably served as an inspiration for Carové when writing the story. By 1830 Runge was no longer well known. Carové's selection thus makes him an early admirer of an artist who today is considered one of the most important of German Romanticism.

In Runge's vignettes the children are sex neutral. Sarah Austin makes *das Kind* to be a boy but her illustrator's, William Harvey's, child is again sex neutral. He has fifteen engravings, one for the title page, one for each of the sections. There are also small decorative engravings at the end of the sections. The reproduction of the title page will give an idea of the rather crowded illustrations, with a child who is often poorly drawn. These engravings were used as "emblems" by A. Bronson Alcott as I mentioned above.

There is one rather undistinguished illustration that accompanies the text of the story in the collection of *Curious Stories* (1856). The artist is Hammet Billings, the engraver John Andrews. The engraving shows a sex neutral child sitting under a bush, with two dragonflies in front.

Except for Frank C. Papé, all of the following artists have placed a pertinent quotation from the text under or above each illustration.

I have selected one of the fourteen color-printed plates by Eleanor Vere Boyle and executed by the Leighton Brothers as a frontispiece for this edition because of its beauty and because I believe that it expresses the spirit of Carové's story better than any of the other illustrations of *The Story Without an End*. The plate refers specifically to the child's dream in section three. Brigid Peppin mentions that the "wonderfully rich effects created by Eleanor Vere Boyle […] involved

[...] no less than twelve separate [wood] blocks."[15] It must be said that some of the fourteen color illustrations are of less quality than the one selected for this volume. Boyle also added a tinted wood-engraved frontispiece that, except for reproducing the title of the story, is strangely unrelated to Carové's text since we see a wall with a youth sitting on it who is holding a large book under the right arm. There are also, in addition to another book, putti, an owl, and in the background a landscape with a church. On the title page is a wood-engraved vignette that is again not related to the story as the vignette shows a child sitting at a table with a plate and a bowl on it. Finally, there are thirteen wood-engraved vignettes in the text. As in the case of William Harvey, Boyle's illustrations show a child of undetermined sex.

In the miniature edition of the story of 1899 (London) we find seven illustrations by Aimée G. Clifford that again show a sex-neutral child with a round face and a sweet expression.

Paul Henry's four illustrations have what seems to be a boy with a rather detailed face and dressed in a piece of cloth draped around his hips.

In the front matter of his edition of 1904 Curtis Wager-Smith carefully describes the contents of each of his nine illustrations as well as the frontispiece which shows "The Child," a rather sweet-looking boy, surrounded by plants and animals. The illustrations give the impression of woodcuts.

The frontispiece and thirteen illustrations by an unknown artist in Thomas Wentworth Higginson's 1902 edition show a fully-dressed boy.

Finally, in 1912, Frank Cheyne Papé added a frontispiece and seven beautifully colored illustrations, most of which show a naked boy in a natural setting that is drawn with much imagination. As in the previous editions, there is a quotation from the text for each illustration, this time on a special transparent sheet preceding the plate, except for the frontispiece where the sheet follows the plate.

I should also mention that several copies of the editions I have seen have elaborate decorative bindings.

---

[15] Brigid Peppin, *Fantasy. The Golden Age of Fantastic Illustration* (New York: Watson Guptill, 1965), p. 8.

Bibliography of the German and English Editions

IN THE FOLLOWING list full bibliographical descriptions are given only for the two primary editions, the ones that form the basis for the texts printed here. The subsequent editions have minimal entries only. The editions are grouped chronologically and according to authors of prefaces, illustrators, and the issues of private presses. Also, if the story formed part of a collection of works, a special group was formed.

After the bibliographical entry the source for the information is given. The following abbreviations are used: BL for *The British Library. General Catalogue of Books to 1975*; BQM for Bayard Quincy Morgan, *A Critical Bibliography of German Literature in English Translation, 1481-1927* (New York and London: Scarecrow Press, 1965, 2nd ed.); NUC for *National Union Catalog of Pre-1956 Imprints*.

If I have seen a copy of the book or a microfilm, that fact is indicated by the abbreviation CES after the library where I saw the book or from which I obtained the microfilm. I use the NUC abbreviations for the various libraries.

In a number of cases the year of publication is uncertain because the title page is missing or torn. These editions are placed at the end of the decade within which they presumably appeared.

German Language Editions

Moosblüthen, zum Christgeschenk von Friedrich Wilhelm Carové. Frankfurt a.M. Druck und Verlag von Heinr. Ludw. Brönner. [1830]. iv, 264.

BL; Staatsbibliothek zu Berlin Preussischer Kulturbesitz (CES).

The date of publication is taken from Carové's preface which is signed "Frankfurt a. M. im Juli 1830. F. W. C." (p. iv). Also from a contemporary review in the *Blätter für literarische Unterhaltung* (1832, Nr. 24, pp. 99-100).

Frontispiece: Christ child by Johannes Valdor and five vignettes by Philipp Otto Runge on unnumbered pages in the text engraved by "Herrn Becker von Darmstadt" (p. iv). The Runge vignette preceding *Kinderleben oder das Mährchen ohne Ende* is on an unnumbered page immediately preceding the text of the story on pp. 27-70.

The Staatsbibliothek zu Berlin Preussischer Kulturbesitz kindly authorized publication of *Kinderleben oder das Mährchen ohne Ende* from a microfilm of their copy which has the following call number: Uz 7181 R.

There are, as already mentioned, German language editions that served instructional purposes: London: Senior, 1841 (Heinrich Apel, ed.); London, Leipzig: Thimm, 1852 (H. Mathias, ed.); New York: Holt, 1864.

English Language Editions

Sarah Austin is the translator in all cases except for a couple of editions listed at the end of this section. I have always transcribed the title of her translation as *The Story Without an End* since bibliographical entries from various sources are unreliable as to capitalization.

1   *The Story Without an End*. From the German of F. W. Carové, By Sarah Austin. Illustrated by William Harvey. [Wood engraving.] London: Published by Effingham Wilson, Royal Exchange. 1834. [viii], 9-[124], [4], [1]-16.

[i] THE STORY WITHOUT AN END [ii] empty [iii] title page, see above [iv] empty [v]-vi TO MY DAUGHTER [vii] empty [viii] wood engraving 9-123 the text [124] Printed by Maurice & Co., Fenchurch Street. [125-28] advertising for "Mrs. Austin's Bible Selections" [1]-16 advertising for other books by the publisher. There are fourteen wood engravings by William Harvey, one preceding each section as well as an ornamental vignette at the end of page 123.

BL (CES); BQM no. 1039; NUC; IU (CES).

1a   As 1, but: [1840?].

BL: Imperfect; PSt (CES). The copy in the Pattee Library of the Pennsylvania State University is probably the same edition as the copy in the BL. Advertising in the PSt copy points toward 1844 as the date of publication.

1b   As 1, but: New and improved edition. London: Virtue Brothers. [1864].

BL (CES); BQM no. 1042.

1c   As 1b, but: Low, Son & Marston. [186-?].

NUC.

1d   As 1, but: Boston: Estes. [1899].

BQM no. 1050; NUC.

1e   As 1, but: New York: Putnam. [190?].

BQM no. 1054 (gives as date of publication 1904 and indicates that it is illustrated); NUC (does not give date of publication; also, no indication as to illustrations).

2   *Story Without an End*; translated from the German of Carove [sic] by Sarah Austin, with a preface and key to the emblems, by A. Bronson Alcott. Boston: Joseph H. Francis; New York: Charles S. Francis, 1836.

BQM no. 1040; NUC; ViU (CES). For a description of Alcott's edition see under "Prefaces."

2a As 2, but: Boston: J. H. Francis, 1848.

MnU (CES); NUC.

2b As 2, but: New York: J. Miller, 1877?

NUC.

2c As 2b, but: [1889?]

NUC.

3   As 1, but: A new edition. To which is added The glow-worm. Translated by Dr. Reich. London: Effingham Wilson, [183?].

NUC.

4   In: *Curious Stories about fairies and other funny people*. With illustrations by Billings. Boston: Ticknor and Fields, 1856.

BL (CES); BQM no. 1041; NUC. *The Story Without an End* is on pp. [237]-266.

5   As 1, but: With illustrations printed in colours after drawings by E. V. B. [Eleanor Vere Boyle]. London: Sampson Low, Son, and Marston, 1868.

BL; BQM no. 1043; NcU (CES); NUC.

5a As 5, but: Sampson Low, Son, and Marston, and Searle, 1872.

BQM no. 1044; NUC; PSt (CES).

5b As 5a, but: 1874.

BL; BQM no. 1045. The entry for an 1879 edition in NUC (0151397) is a mistake.

6   Peter Schlemihl by Adelbert Chamisso. The Story Without an End by Carodé [sic]. Hymns to Night by Novalis. London, Paris & Melbourne: Cassell, 1889.

BL; BQM no. C492; NUC. Philipp Rath, *Bibliotheca Schlemihliana. Ein Verzeichnis der Ausgaben und Übersetzungen des Peter Schlemihl*. Berlin: Breslauer, 1919, no. 128.

6a As 6, but: Philadelphia: Altemus, ca. 1899.

Rath no. 132.

6b As 6a, but: [1899] and with illustrations.

Rath no. 133.

6c As 6a, but: 1907?

NUC.

7   As 1, but: Portland, Me.: T. B. Mosher, 1897.

NcD; NUC. Benton L. Hatch, *A Check List of the Publications of Thomas Bird Mosher of Portland, Maine*. University of Massachusetts, 1966, no. 45 (August 1897).

7a As 7, but December 1897 according to Hatch no. 61.

7b As 7, but: 1900.

BQM no. 1052; Hatch no. 172; NUC.

7c As 7, but: 1904.

Hatch no. 308; NUC. A 1907 edition of 7 (NUC 0151407) does not exist.

8   As 1, but: With illustrations by Aimée G. Clifford. London: Wells Gardner Darton, 1899.

BL (CES); BQM no. 1051.

9   As 1, but: With a preface by Thomas Wentworth Higginson: with fourteen illustrations. Boston: Heath, 1902.

BQM no. 1053; NUC; OrU (CES). The notation in NUC (0151404) that the illustration are "after the drawings by E. V. B." is incorrect; there is no resemblance between the two sets of illustrations.

9a As 9, but: 1909.

Dacus Library, Winthrop College, Rock Hill, S.C. (CES); NUC. According to *The Publishers' Trade List Annual* Heath had the book in its catalogue as late as 1935. I was informed that the 1934 copy, listed in the NUC (0151410) as being at the Cleveland Public Library, is not at that library.

10 As 1, but: With illustrations and an introduction by Curtis Wager-Smith. Philadelphia: Altemus, 1904.

BQM no. 1055; NUC.

11 As 1, but: Illustrated by Paul Henry. London: Duckworth, 1904.

BL (CES); BQM no. 1056.

12 As 1, but: Ashendene Press, 1909.

BL (CES). Preceding the title page there is a dedication "To Diana, on the occasion of her ninth birthday, from the Printer, Greeting." P. 60: "Printed for Diana Hornby on her ninth birthday by her father, St John Hornby, at the Ashendene Press, Shelley House, Chelsea, the fifteenth day of May, 1909." No. 23 of *A Descriptive Bibliography of the Books Printed at the Ashendene Press MDCCCXCV-MCMXXXV*. Shelley House, Chelsea, 1935 (rpt. 1976).

13 As 1, but: With illustrations by Frank C. Papé. London: Duckworth, 1912.

BL; BQM no. 1057; PSt.

13a As 13, but: New York: Duffield, 1913.

BQM no. 1058; NcU (CES).

As I mentioned above, J. C. Pickard also translated Carové's *Kinderleben oder das Mährchen ohne Ende* and kept Sarah Austin's title. Chicago: Winchell, [1885]. BQM no. 1046; NN (CES); NUC. B. Q. Morgan also lists an 1886-1887 edition: With the palace of vanity; from the French. Boston, Chicago: Interstate. BQM no. 1047.